BEST OF TURKISH COOKING

Published by Tughra Books
345 Clifton Ave., Clifton,
NJ, 07011, USA

www.tughrabooks.com

Editors: Ali Budak, Ruth Woodhall, Korkut Altay

Recipes: Gülnur Aygün, Yeşim Kurtuluş,
        Aver Can, Bahar Karamehmetoğlu,
        İnci Kızılkaya, Nurgün Uçkunkaya,

Translated from Turkish by Pınar Hilal Vurucu

Art Director: Engin Çiftçi

Graphic Design: Şaban Kalyoncu, Erhan Kara

Photographs: Murat Kurtuluş

ISBN: 978-1-59784-209-9

Printed by
Imak Ofset, Istanbul - Turkey

BEST OF TURKISH COOKING

SELECTIONS FROM CONTEMPORARY TURKISH CUISINE

TUGHRA
BOOKS

New Jersey

CONTENTS

Introduction

Surfing through the internet, you may come across people telling others how they enjoyed the food when visiting Turkey and that they are looking for the recipe. Although tastes differ, the diversity of Turkish cuisine means that there is a good chance that it will appeal to you as well. When Prince Charles visited Turkey, he particularly liked one of my favorite dishes: the eggplant salad, or rather, the "aubergine" salad.

If you are interested in healthy food, there are various delicious Mediterranean recipes with fresh vegetables, including dishes made with lashings of olive oil. Desserts? You will most probably be surprised to see how simple recipes make lovely desserts, for example the quince or pumpkin dessert recipe. While investigating whether different types of pumpkins are suitable for this syrupy dessert, one of the Turkish staff members related how they had amazed their American friends with the delicious dessert made from the Halloween pumpkin.

Willing to have a deeper gastronomic experience? We hope that the dishes once pleased the Ottoman sultans will please you as well. Ottoman culinary culture had the advantage of a multinational background and the recipes were perfected in the palace kitchens to please the sultan. The palace chefs plundered the market to come up with new dishes to receive imperial praises. It is reported that they made more than a hundred different dishes with eggplants. Many of the extremely elaborate recipes have now been forgotten, but the origins of many tasty dishes in modern Turkish cooking, such as imam bayildi, have their origins in the Ottoman traditions. This humorous name is literally translated as "the imam fainted," but a more correct translation would be "the imam took great delight in it."

Most Turkish kebab houses in different parts of the world serve the cuisine of Southeast Anatolia. These dishes are also common in neighboring Middle Eastern cuisines. Different ethnic groups claim the most popular ones as their own, such as döner kebab (gyros) or baklava. No matter who invented baklava first, this Anatolian delight is difficult to make; the recipe we give here is a more practical version.

If you ever have Turkish neighbors, do not be surprised when they knock your door and offer you a bowl of ashure (Noah's pudding) or some other dessert like lokma; it is likely to be on one of their festive days. Encouraged by the Prophet Muhammad, neighborliness and sharing food is an important aspect of the social culture. Particularly in Ramadan people invite their friends and relatives to break the fast with them. During the Eid al-Adha (Festival of Sacrifice) Prophet Abraham is also commemorated. Prophet Abraham was famous for his generosity and everybody was welcome at his table. In the same way that Turkish guests invoke God's blessings for the host when they get up from the table, we also wish: "May God grant Abraham's abundance to your table."

Bon appetite/Afiyet olsun!

SOUPS

TOMATO SOUP
(SERVES 4)

INGREDIENTS

1/3 cup rice
2 tbsp butter
2 tbsp flour
1.5 cups warm water
1.5 cups milk
1 tbsp tomato paste
3 tomatoes, skinned and grated
salt
black pepper
dried mint
4 tbsp grated cheese

PREPARATION:

Boil the rice (in a cup of water)

Meanwhile, melt the butter and slowly add flour, stirring with a wooden spoon until flour becomes slightly golden. Slowly add the warm water and milk, stirring well to avoid lumps.

Mix the tomato paste with a small amount of water, and add to the pan along with the tomatoes. Add the salt and the rice and continue to cook over a low heat for 10–15 minutes.

Remove from the heat. Garnish with black pepper, mint, and cheese. Serve.

EZOGELİN SOUP
(SERVES 6)

INGREDIENTS

1 onion
1 tbsp oil
2 tbsp tomato paste
1 tbsp sweet or hot red pepper paste
9 cups water or beef stock
1/3 cup fine bulgur wheat
1/3 cup red lentils
1/3 cup rice
1 tbsp vermicelli
salt and pepper
2 tbsp butter, melted
1 (or 1/2) teaspoon of red hot pepper
2 tsp dry mint

PREPARATION:

Fry onions in oil until golden. Blend tomato paste with a little water and add to the pan. Add red pepper paste and stir. Add six cups of water or stock and bring to the boil on a medium heat.

When it comes to the boil, add the bulgur, red lentils, rice, vermicelli, black pepper and salt. Boil the soup until the grains are very tender.

Remove from the heat and place in bowls. Garnish with melted butter with hot pepper and, dry mint before serving.

COLLARD SOUP
(SERVES 4)

INGREDIENTS

1 onion, chopped
2 tbsp butter
1 bunch of collard greens, finely chopped
8 cups beef stock
2/3 cup corn flour
3 cloves garlic, finely chopped
1/2 cup boiled borlotti beans
2/3 cup canned corn
1 tsp salt
1 tsp red pepper flakes

PREPARATION:

Soften the onion in 1 tablespoon of the butter. Add the chopped greens and continue to fry until foam is formed. Add the beef stock, and then the corn flour, and stir.

Cook on a low heat and add the garlic, boiled beans and corn a few minutes before you take the soup off the heat. Add salt to taste and heat through before serving.

To garnish the soup, heat the remaining butter and the pepper flakes until sizzling. Pour a little onto the surface of the soup in each bowl.

TARHANA SOUP WITH MEATBALLS
(SERVES 4)

INGREDIENTS

4 tbsp tarhana powder (see note below)
4 cups water
8 oz/200 g ground beef
1 onion, finely chopped
salt and pepper
2 tbsp butter
1 tsp dried mint leaves
1 tsp red pepper flakes

PREPARATION:

Mix the 4 tablespoons of tarhana powder with 4 cups of water. Leave to stand for 10 minutes.

Meanwhile, combine the ground beef, onion, salt and pepper to make a meatball mix. Roll tiny meatballs which are slightly larger than garbanzo beans. (Wet your hands with cold water to stop the mixture sticking.) Dry fry the meatballs in a non-stick pan.

In a large pan bring the tarhana and water mixture to the boil. Add the meatballs and boil for 5 minutes. Remove from the heat.

In a separate pan, heat the butter, mint, and red pepper flakes. Pour the sizzling mix onto the surface of the soup and serve.

Note: Tarhana is a powder made of dried curds and flour. It is used as a base for soup

---

LEMON CHICKEN SOUP
(SERVES 4)

INGREDIENTS

1/2 chicken breast
4 cups water
2 tbsp butter
2 tbsp flour
1 pint/1/2 liter chicken stock
juice of 2 lemons
yolks of 2 eggs
salt
2 cloves garlic, crushed
red pepper flakes

PREPARATION:

Boil the chicken breast in 4 cups of water, and drain, reserving the stock. Allow the chicken to cool and then shred it. Meanwhile, beat the egg yolks and lemon juice together well.

Melt the butter and add the flour, stirring constantly with a wooden spoon to make sure it does not become lumpy. Add in the stock reserved from boiling the chicken and top up with as much extra stock as you think necessary. Simmer and stir constantly to prevent lumps. Add the shredded chicken. Stir the egg yolk and lemon juice mixture into the soup slowly. Add the salt and crushed garlic.

Pour into serving bowls and garnish with red pepper flakes.

TRICOLOR PASTA SOUP
(SERVES 2)

INGREDIENTS

1 cup tricolor pasta, boiled
half a cup boiled cannellini beans
1 red bell pepper, sliced thinly
1/2 chicken breast, boiled and cubed
1 carrot, grated
2 garlic cloves, finely chopped
2 tbsp oil
6 cups water
1 tbsp red pepper paste
2 tbsp flour

PREPARATION:

Heat the oil in a large pan. Add the garlic and onions and fry lightly until translucent. Add the carrot and red pepper and continue to fry until soft. Add the water and bring to the boil.

Add the cooked beans, chicken, and pasta. Simmer for 15 minutes.

Remove one cup of the soup, and whisk this with the red pepper paste and flour. Beat this mixture slowly and thoroughly back into the soup. Cook for another 2–3 minutes.

Serve hot.

VEGETABLE SOUP
(SERVES 2)

INGREDIENTS

1 onion, finely chopped
1 clove of garlic, finely chopped
1 leek, finely chopped
1 carrot, finely chopped
1 zucchini, finely chopped
oil
6 cups water
2 tbsp flour
1 egg
2 tbsp yogurt
red pepper flakes
a sprig of parsley, finely chopped

PREPARATION:

Fry all the vegetables in a large pan. Add the water and bring to the boil. Leave to simmer.

Whisk the flour, egg and yogurt with a little water. When the vegetables in the soup are tender, stir in the flour, egg and yogurt mixture. Sprinkle with pepper flakes and parsley to serve.

WEDDING SOUP
(SERVES 2)

INGREDIENTS

10 oz/250 g lamb meat, cubed
6 cups beef stock
2 tbsp flour
4 tbsp yogurt
salt
2 tbsp butter
1 tsp pepper flakes
1.5 tsp. tomato paste

PREPARATION:

Put the lamb in a large pan with a small amount of water and bring to the boil. Add the remaining water and continue to boil until the meat is tender.

In a bowl, whisk the flour and yogurt together. Take a cupful of the beef stock and stir this into the flour and yogurt mix.

Slowly add this to the boiling stock and meat in the large pan, whisking throughout. Bring back to the boil, and add salt to taste.

In a separate pan, fry the red pepper flakes and tomato paste in the butter until they sizzle. Pour over the soup before serving. Serve hot.

SUMMER YOGURT SOUP
(SERVES 2)

INGREDIENTS

1 cup coarse whole wheat grains, washed and soaked overnight
6 cups beef stock
1.5 tsp salt
400 g of yogurt
5 cups cold water
1 tsp red pepper flakes
1/3 cup oil
ice cubes
1 tbsp dried mint

PREPARATION:

Boil the wheat grains in 6 cups of water or beef stock until tender. Add salt and leave to cool. Once the wheat has been fully cooled, add the yogurt and stir well. Add 5 cups of cold water and stir. Pour into the serving bowls.

Heat the red pepper flakes in the oil. Drizzle on the top of the soup. Add an ice cube or two to each bowl. Garnish with a sprinkling of dried mint.

RUMELI-STYLE TRIPE SOUP
(SERVES 4)

INGREDIENTS

2 lb/1 kg fresh calf tripe
8 pints/5 liters water
1/2 oz/10 g salt
juice of half a lemon
2 cloves of garlic
1 onion, chopped
2 tbsp butter
red pepper flakes
vinegar

PREPARATION:

Clean the tripe well. Scrape the inner and outer sides well with a knife on a cutting board. Discard any parts that cannot be cleaned properly. Wash the tripe in lukewarm water. Put it in a very large pan with the salt, lemon juice, the chopped garlic clove, and onion. Add the water and boil hard for 2.5–3 hours. From time to time remove any foam that gathers on the surface of the water in the pan.

Remove the pan from the heat and allow to cool. Reserve the stock in the pan, and once the tripe is cold, cut it into 1/2 inch (1cm) cubes. Take 4 pints (about 2 liters) of the reserved stock and pour it over the cubed tripe. Cook on a low heat for 5–10 minutes more.

Remove from heat and pour into serving bowls. Melt the butter in a small pan and add the red pepper flakes. Drizzle over the soup. After serving, a few dashes of vinegar can be added to.

SALADS

BEAN SALAD
(SERVES 4-6)

INGREDIENTS

1 can of cannellini or navy beans
1 can of borlotti beans
1 yellow bell pepper, diced
1 red bell pepper, diced

DRESSING:

1 tbsp vinegar
2 tbsp olive oil
juice of 1 lemon
salt to taste
3 green onions, finely chopped

PREPARATION:

Wash and drain both the beans. In a deep bowl mix the beans with the diced peppers. Whisk the dressing ingredients, add to the salad and toss well. Garnish with the finely chopped green onions and serve.

Note: For best results, after adding the dressing, leave to stand for 2 hours before garnishing and serving.

SPRING SALAD
(SERVES 10)

INGREDIENTS

6 medium-sized potatoes
2 carrots
half a bunch of fresh dill
half a bunch of green onions
pickles (pickled cucumbers)
3 tbsp mayonnaise

DRESSING:

3 tbsp mayonnaise
1 tbsp yogurt
salt to taste
olives
yolks of 2 boiled eggs

PREPARATION:

Boil the potatoes and mash them well. After the potatoes have cooled, add salt and three tablespoons of mayonnaise and mix. Divide the potatoes and mayonnaise mixture into two halves. Grate the carrots into one of the halves, and mix well. Next, chop the pickles, green onions and dill, add to the remaining half of the potato and mayonnaise mixture, and mix well.

Construct the salad in three layers. Put half of the mixture with carrots into a deep bowl or mold, pressing down well to flatten the surface. On top of this lay all of the mixture with pickles, onions, and dill, and press flat again. Make a top layer with the remaining carrot mixture and press down to flatten. Leave the salad in the bowl to cool in the refrigerator for at least 3 hours.

To serve, invert the bowl or mold and turn the salad out onto a serving dish. Fold a tablespoon of yogurt into three tablespoons of mayonnaise. Pour onto the top of the salad. Push the cooked egg yolks through a metal sieve and sprinkle over the mayonnaise topping. Garnish with olives.

BLACK-EYED PEA SALAD
(SERVES 4-6)

INGREDIENTS

10 oz/250 g black-eyed peas
half a bunch of fresh dill, chopped
half a bunch of parsley, chopped
2 grilled red peppers, finely chopped
2 green cayenne (or milder) peppers, finely chopped
6 green onions
10 pickled gherkins, finely chopped
1 cup boiled corn

DRESSING:

half a cup olive oil
1 lemon
1 tbsp vinegar
2 cloves garlic, crushed
1 tsp salt

PREPARATION:

Soak the black-eyed peas overnight, then rinse, drain, and boil until tender. Wash and drain them and place in a deep bowl. Add dill, parsley, red and green pepper, green onions, pickles and corn. Mix well.

Whisk the olive oil, lemon, vinegar, garlic and salt to make the dressing. Pour over the salad. Toss well.

Note: Prepare two hours before serving for best results.

SAUSAGE AND PASTA SALAD
(SERVES 6)

INGREDIENTS

250 g bowtie pasta.
5 oz /140 g sausage, boiled and chopped
2 bell green peppers, julienned
1 cup cooked peas
3–4 green onions, finely chopped
4–5 small pickles, diced
2 tomatoes, diced
8–10 green olives, halved
1 carrot, grated
half a bunch of fresh dill, chopped
half a bunch of parsley, chopped

DRESSING:

3–4 cloves garlic, crushed
1 cup yogurt
1 cup mayonnaise

PREPARATION:

Boil pasta until al dente. Drain, place in large bowl, and add chopped sausages, salami, peppers, peas, green onions, pickles, tomatoes, olives, dill, and parsley. Mix well.

Combine yogurt, mayonnaise, crushed garlic and salt. Stir into salad mixture and serve.

CAULIFLOWER SALAD
(SERVES 6)

INGREDIENTS

1 mid-sized cauliflower

DRESSING:

3 cups yogurt
3 cloves garlic, crushed
half a cup finely chopped walnuts
3 tbsp mayonnaise
2 tsp salt
2 tbsp melted butter
1 tbsp tomato paste
5–6 cherry tomatoes, halved
5–6 sprigs of parsley, chopped

PREPARATION:

Remove the root and leaves from the cauliflower. Add enough water to a pan to immerse the cauliflower entirely. Then add a teaspoon of salt and boil it for fifteen minutes. Drain, cool slightly and separate into large pieces on serving dish.

Whisk the yogurt with garlic, walnuts, mayonnaise and salt. Pour the yogurt sauce over the cauliflower florets. Mix tomato paste and butter. Pour over the yogurt dressing. Garnish the salad with cherry tomatoes, sprinkle with finely chopped parsley, and serve.

CRACKED WHEAT SALAD (KISIR)
(POUR 6 PERSONNES)

INGREDIENTS

2 cups fine bulgur wheat
2 cups boiling water

DRESSING:

3 tbsp oil
juice of 1 lemon
1 tbsp sour pomegranate paste
2 tbsp tomato paste
2 tbsp red pepper paste
salt
pepper
2 tomatoes, diced
1 cucumber, diced
3–4 green onions, finely chopped
1/2 bunch of parsley, finely chopped
red pepper flakes
6 lettuce leaves

PREPARATION:

Pour boiling water over the bulgur wheat and leave to stand in a covered bowl for about 15 minutes. When the bulgur wheat has absorbed all the water, leave to cool for a few more minutes. Add the oil, lemon juice, pomegranate paste, tomato paste, red pepper paste, salt, and pepper, and knead the mixture thoroughly. Allow the bulgur wheat to absorb the dressing. Add diced tomatoes, cucumbers, green onions, parsley, and pepper flakes, mixing all ingredients well with the bulgur wheat. Serve the salad on a bed of lettuce leaves on a large flat dish or in six individual servings on lettuce leaves.

Note: Dill, mint and basil can also be added as desired.

MUSHROOM SALAD
(SERVES 4)

INGREDIENTS

12 oz/400 g mushrooms
6–7 dill pickles
2 long green cayenne (or milder) peppers.
1 cup canned corn

DRESSING:

juice of 1 lemon
half a cup olive oil
salt to taste
half a bunch of fresh dill, finely chopped
1 sprig of parsley, finely chopped
cherry tomatoes, halved

PREPARATION:

Wash mushrooms and boil for 2–3 minutes, drain and leave to cool. Meanwhile, slice the dill pickles lengthwise and julienne the peppers. When the mushrooms have been boiled, slice them and place in a bowl. Add the pickles, peppers, corn, lemon juice, olive oil and salt, and toss all the ingredients well. Place in a serving dish and garnish with dill, parsley and cherry tomatoes.

Note: Canned mushrooms can be used as well

RED LENTIL BALLS
(SERVES 8-10)

INGREDIENTS

1.5 cups fine bulgur wheat
2 cups red lentils
olive oil for frying
7 green onions chopped
1 onion, grated
2 tomatoes, grated
1 tsp salt
1 tsp black pepper
1 tsp cumin
1 tsp red pepper flakes
half a bunch parsley, finely chopped
lemon wedges
green onions
tomatoes, sliced

PREPARATION:

Boil the red lentils in plenty of water. After they begin to soften, turn off the heat, add the bulgur wheat and allow the mixture to stand for twenty minutes with the lid closed. Meanwhile, fry the onions in a pan with olive oil until translucent. Add the tomatoes and continue to fry for 2 more minutes. Add the onion and tomato mix to the bulgur wheat and lentils (you can also add some tomato paste if you wish). Add salt and other spices, knead by hand for 10 minutes. Add the parsley last and knead again.

Break walnut-sized pieces from the mix and shape into small balls by rolling in the palm of your hand. Place the balls on a serving dish. Garnish with lemon wedges, green onions and tomato slices.

Note: You can add crushed walnuts with the lentils if desired.

LENTIL AND PASTA SALAD
(SERVES 8)

INGREDIENTS

1 cup green lentils
10 oz/250 g pasta
4–5 green onions.
1 bunch of fresh dill
1 bunch of parsley
1 red bell pepper
2–3 dill pickles
2–3 tbsp canned corn

DRESSING:

salt
red pepper flakes
oil
fresh mint, chopped

PREPARATION:

Boil the green lentils and pasta separately and drain. Meanwhile, finely chop the dill, onions and parsley. Slice the red pepper and dill pickles. Mix all the ingredients in a deep serving dish. Dress with salt, oil, and pepper flakes and garnish with mint leaves before serving.

SEASONAL SALAD
(SERVES 4-6)

INGREDIENTS

half a red cabbage, cut into small strips
juice of 1 lemon
salt
1 iceberg lettuce, quartered
2 carrots, grated
3–4 tbsp canned corn
half a bunch of garden rocket
half a bunch of parsley

DRESSING:

lemon juice
olive oil
feta cheese or croutons

PREPARATION:

Place red cabbage strips in a bowl, add salt and lemon juice and mix well, using your hand.

1. Arrange the lettuce quarters on a serving dish, like the petals of a flower. Scatter the cabbage strips and grated carrot all around the lettuce. Scatter the corn over the top of the cabbage and carrots. Arrange the garden rocket and parsley leaves in the middle of the serving dish. Drizzle the lemon juice and olive oil over the top and add the garnish (if used) before serving.

POTATO SALAD
(SERVES 5)

INGREDIENTS

2 lb/1 kg small new potatoes
2 medium-sized onions, halved and sliced
1 tomato, diced
half a bunch of parsley, finely chopped
1 lettuce, cut into thin strips

DRESSING:

juice of half a lemon
four tbsp. vinegar
1/3 cup oil
salt to taste

PREPARATION:

Boil the new potatoes and slip the skins off. Cut each potato in half (or quarters if they are larger) and place them in a large bowl. Wash the onions in a sieve, squeezing them slightly, then add to the bowl with the potatoes. Now add the diced tomato, finely chopped parsley and lettuce and mix well. Whisk the dressing ingredients together. Drizzle over the top and serve.

GRILLED EGGPLANT SALAD
(SERVES 6)

INGREDIENTS

6 medium-sized eggplants
3 tomatoes, diced
5–6 green cayenne (or milder) peppers, diced
1 onion, cut into rings
1 cucumber, chopped finely
3 green onions, finely chopped
1/2 bunch of parsley, finely chopped
1/2 bunch of fresh mint, finely chopped
3–4 cloves garlic, crushed

DRESSING:

1/2 cup oil
1 lemon or 3–4 tbsp vinegar
1 tsp salt

PREPARATION:

Grill the eggplants or roast them in the oven, and peel them. Puree the eggplants and mix with all the other ingredients. Whisk the dressing ingredients, mix with the salad and serve.

POTATO SALAD WITH GARDEN ROCKET SAUCE
(SERVES 8)

INGREDIENTS

8 medium-sized potatoes, boiled and cubed
lettuce, thinly sliced (optional)
carrot, grated (optional)

DRESSING:

1 cup yogurt
2 tbsp mayonnaise
half a bunch of garden rocket, finely chopped
half a bunch of parsley, finely chopped
2 cloves garlic, crushed
salt to taste
red pepper flakes (optional)

PREPARATION:

Mix the dressing ingredients in a large bowl. Add the cubed, boiled potatoes (and other salad ingredients, if used) and mix well. Place in a serving dish. Allow to cool in refrigerator for 1 hour before serving.

WATERCRESS SALAD
(SERVES 2)

INGREDIENTS

1 bunch of watercress (or purslane, if available), roughly chopped
2 roasted red bell peppers, sliced

DRESSING:

2–3 tbsp olive oil
juice of 1 lemon
1 tsp salt
1 handful of chopped walnuts

PREPARATION:

Put the roughly chopped watercress into a salad bowl. Scatter the sliced peppers on top.

Whisk the olive oil, lemon juice and salt together and pour over the salad ingredients. Garnish with walnuts and serve.

Note: It is easiest to use pre-roasted peppers for this dish if you can find them. However, if you decide to roast the peppers yourself, it is also possible to freeze some for later use.

POTATO BALLS WITH YOGURT
(SERVES 8)

INGREDIENTS

8 medium-sized potatoes
half a bunch of parsley
half a bunch of fresh dill
salt
pepper

DRESSING:

1 cup yogurt
2 cloves of garlic crushed

GARNISH:

1/3 cup olive oil
1 tsp paprika
1 tsp red pepper flakes

PREPARATION:

Boil potatoes, mash, and leave to cool. Add parsley, dill and and seasonings to taste; knead. Break off egg-sized pieces and roll into balls. (Dip your hand into water so the potato balls do not stick to your hands.) Arrange the balls on a serving dish.

Whisk the yogurt and garlic. Pour the dressing over the potato balls.

In a small pan, fry the paprika and red pepper flakes in olive oil. Drizzle this garnish over the yogurt dressing and serve.

SAUTÉED PEPPERS WITH OLIVE OIL
(SERVES 2)

INGREDIENTS

2 red bell peppers
2 green bell peppers
2 green cayenne (or milder) peppers
2–3 cloves garlic, crushed
half a cup olive oil
1 zucchini, julienned
2 hot peppers, cut into rings
3 tomatoes, diced
4–5 green onions, sliced
1 tsp soy sauce
salt to taste

PREPARATION:

Roast the red peppers and green bell peppers until blackened. Peel them and cut into thin strips. Fry the garlic in olive oil. Add the zucchini and fry together. Add the cayenne peppers, tomatoes, and onions, frying for another 5 minutes Add the soy sauce and salt, and stir for another 1–2 minutes. Remove from the heat and allow to cool before serving.

Note: If you drop the peppers into a bowl of cold water immediately after roasting them (while they are still hot), the skins will lift off more easily.

CARROT SALAD
(SERVES 2-3)

INGREDIENTS

1 lb/500 g carrots, grated
2 tbsp olive oil
2 cloves garlic, finely chopped
2 tsp cumin
1 tsp red pepper flakes
1 tbsp red pepper paste
1 tsp sugar
salt
3 tbsp finely chopped parsley
juice of 1 lemon
parsley, finely chopped

PREPARATION:

Heat the oil and fry the garlic for 2–3 minutes. Add cumin, red pepper flakes, red pepper paste, sugar, and salt, and mix. Add parsley and lemon juice and mix again. Then add 1 cup of the grated carrots and cook for 3–5 minutes.

Remove the mixture from the heat, add the remaining uncooked, grated carrot, and leave to cool. Let the carrot salad sit in the fridge for at least 1 hour, garnish with finely chopped parsley, and serve.

WHITE BEAN SALAD
(SERVES 5)

INGREDIENTS

10 oz/250 g dried cannellini or navy beans
1 cup vinegar
1 large onion, halved and sliced
2 green bell peppers, sliced
1 bunch of parsley, finely chopped

DRESSING:

6 tbsp olive oil
2 tbsp vinegar
salt

GARNISH:

2 medium tomatoes, sliced
2 boiled eggs, sliced
parsley, finely chopped

PREPARATION:

Soak the beans in cold water overnight. Drain, and place in a pan, covering with water, and bring to the boil. Cook on a low heat until the beans are tender. Remove some of the water from the pot and leave the beans to cool. Drain the beans and place in a deep bowl. Add one cup of vinegar, cover, and allow to rest for two hours. Drain the beans. Place in a serving dish. Add the sliced onions, peppers and parsley, and mix.

Whisk the dressing ingredients together and pour over the bean. Garnish with slices of boiled egg and tomato, and sprinkle with parsley to serve.

GREEN OLIVE SALAD
(SERVES 2 - 3)

INGREDIENTS

1 cup green olives, sliced
2 tbsp fresh dill
2 tbsp parsley
3 green onions
4 large mushrooms, diced

DRESSING:

1 tbsp pomegranate paste
2 tbsp olive oil
juice of one lemon
salt to taste

PREPARATION:

Whisk the pomegranate paste with the olive oil, lemon juice and salt in a bowl. Add the green olives, dill, parsley, and green onions and mix well. Add the diced mushrooms and stir. Serve.

GARBANZO BEAN SALAD
(SERVES 8-10)

INGREDIENTS

2 leeks, green and white parts, sliced
1 lb/500 g potatoes, cubed and boiled
12 oz/400 g of tomatoes, cubed
3 cloves garlic, crushed
1 lb/500 g garbanzo beans, cooked

DRESSING:

5–6 tbsp lemon juice
2 tbsp soy sauce or pomegranate paste
half a bunch of parsley, finely chopped
4–5 sprigs of mint, finely chopped
1 tsp lemon zest
black pepper and salt
tomato cubes
leek rings
mint
parsley

PREPARATION:

Cube the tomatoes and potatoes, cutting them to roughly the same size. Set aside a little bit of the tomatoes and some leek rings to use later in the garnish. Set aside some mint leaves and parsley for the garnish before mincing the rest.

Boil the sliced leeks in salted water for 2 minutes and drain.

Combine all the dressing ingredients

Mix the cubed and boiled potatoes, the leeks, the remaining tomatoes, and the garbanzo beans, pour the salad dressing over them. Leave to rest for 30 minutes.

Move salad to a serving dish and garnish with the tomato cubes, leek rings, mint and parsley you set aside earlier.

VEGETABLE
DISHES

BEAN BORANI
(SERVES 2)

INGREDIENTS

1 lb/500 g fresh green beans
1 cup Turkish style (plain) yogurt
3–4 cloves garlic, crushed
salt
2 tbsp butter
red pepper flakes

PREPARATION:

Top and tail the beans and cut into 2 or 3 pieces. Boil in a small amount of water until tender, remove from heat, and drain.

Add a small amount of water to the yogurt and whisk until it is the consistency of pouring cream. Add the crushed garlic and salt, and stir. Pour over the beans. Place the beans on serving plates.

Melt the butter and add the red pepper flakes. Allow to sizzle. Drizzle over the bean borani and serve immediately.

BEANS WITH PASTRAMI
(SERVES 4)

INGREDIENTS

1 tbsp olive oil
1 tbsp butter
1 medium onion, finely chopped
1 lb/500 g boiled cannellini beans
7–8 slices of pastrami, cut into small pieces
2 bell peppers
2 tbsp tomato paste
salt
black pepper
red pepper flakes

PREPARATION:

Melt butter and oil in a pan. Add onion and fry until slightly golden. Add tomato paste and continue to fry. Add pastrami. Cook over a low heat with the onions for 2–3 minutes. Add the beans, 1.5 cups of boiling water, salt, black pepper, and red pepper flakes. Cook over a medium heat until the flavors have blended. Serve.

Note: Pastrami is being used in the place of a meat product made with spicy, pressed and dried beef (pastirma). It is always cut into thin slices. Sujuk (or any kind of spicy beef sausage) can also be used in this dish instead of the pastrami. In Turkey, this dish is most often cooked with cannellini beans, but you can use any kind of beans for this recipe—borlotti beans, haricot, pinto, etc.

STEWED BEANS WITH PICKLES
(SERVES 6)

INGREDIENTS

1 lb/500 g lamb meat, cubed
1.5 cups cannellini beans
2 tbsp tomato paste
1 tbsp red pepper paste
3 tbsp butter
2 onions
1 soup bowl full of tomato pickles
1 tbsp dried mint
salt to taste

PREPARATION:

Soak beans in water overnight. Boil them in plenty of water until tender and then drain. Dry fry the meat in a pan. Once it has released its own juices, add the finely chopped onions and oil, and fry all together. Add the tomato paste and red pepper paste and remove from the heat when the mixture begins to sizzle.

Add the boiled beans to the meat, followed by 2 cups of water and stir thoroughly. Remove to an oven dish. Garnish the surface with mint, sliced tomatoes, and tomato pickles. Cover with aluminum foil. Bake at 200 °C (390 °F) for 45 minutes. Serve hot.

SPINACH POCKETS
(SERVES 6)

INGREDIENTS

1 lb/500 g spinach, finely sliced
1.5 cups rice
salt
10 oz/250 g feta cheese, crumbled
1 cup mild cheddar cheese, grated
1 egg, beaten (for mix)
3 eggs, beaten (for coating)
half a cup green onions, grated
1 tbsp fresh dill, finely chopped
1 clove garlic, crushed
2 cups dried breadcrumbs,
oil for frying

PREPARATION:

Boil the spinach for 5 minutes and drain. Cook the rice in salted boiling water until it is cooked. Drain and wash with cold water to remove starch.

Mix together the spinach, cooked rice, feta cheese, grated cheese, eggs, green onions, dill, and garlic. Dipping your hands into water each time so the mixture does not stick to them, form the mixture into 18 walnut-sized balls. Roll these into cylinders in your palms. Line the spinach pockets up on a tray and allow to cool in the refrigerator for 30 minutes; this will make the mixture firmer.

Pour the breadcrumbs into a tray. Dip the pockets into the beaten egg and then roll in the bread crumbs, shaking off any excess breadcrumbs. Leave in the refrigerator for another half hour.

Heat the oil in a pan. Fry the spinach pockets until they turn golden brown. Place on kitchen paper to drain excess oil.

Place on a serving dish and serve warm.

STUFFED ZUCCHINI
(SERVES 5)

INGREDIENTS

2 lb/1 kg zucchini
3 onions, cut into rings
1/2 cup oil
8–10 cloves garlic
3 tomatoes, skinned and diced
salt
2 tsp sugar
half a bunch of fresh dill, finely chopped

PREPARATION:

Peel the zucchini, slice them down the middle, but not all the way through, hollowing out the center, like a canoe; remove all the seeds. Wash them and line them up on a tray.

Fry the onions in the oil until they become slightly pink. Add the garlic, tomatoes, salt and sugar and stir together. Fill the zucchini with this mixture. Add a cup of hot water and cook on medium heat until the zucchini are tender. Once the zucchini has cooled off, garnish with dill and serve.

CAULIFLOWER PATTIES
(SERVES 4)

INGREDIENTS

1 small cauliflower
1 tsp vinegar
1 cup water
1 bunch fresh green onions, finely chopped
3 cloves garlic, crushed
4 oz/100 g feta cheese, crumbled
1/2 bunch of fresh dill, finely chopped
1/2 bunch of parsley, finely chopped
2 eggs
3 tbsp flour
salt
black pepper

PREPARATION:

Boil or steam the cauliflower in the vinegar and water. After cooling, separate into small flowerets.

Mix the feta cheese, garlic, eggs, flour, salt and black pepper in a deep bowl. Add the cauliflower, green onions, parsley and dill and mix to coat in the batter.

Heat the oil and drop large spoonfuls of the cauliflower and batter mix into the pan, adding sufficient oil to fry as necessary. Remove each patty when it is golden brown, and drain on kitchen paper.

Serve hot.

RED PEPPER ROLLS
(SERVES 4)

INGREDIENTS

6 red peppers
3 potatoes, boiled
4 tbsp mayonnaise
1 tsp red pepper flakes
salt
8–10 pickled gherkin
1 tbsp lemon juice
1 espresso cup olive oil
a few sprigs of parsley

PREPARATION:

Roast the red peppers until their skins are blackened. Drop into cold water to loosen the skins, then peel them, and remove the seeds. Divide each pepper into two pieces lengthwise.

Grate the boiled potatoes. Add the mayonnaise, red pepper flakes and salt, and mix. Mince the pickles and add to the potato mix.

Put a small amount of the mix on the larger end of each pepper and roll up. Whisk together the lemon juice and olive oil.

Line the rolls up on a serving plate. Drizzle the oil and lemon dressing over the rolls. Garnish with parsley before serving.

ARTICHOKE WITH EGGPLANT PUREE
(SERVES 4)

INGREDIENTS

6–7 artichokes
1 tsp salt
1 tsp sugar
juice of 1 lemon
1 onion, finely chopped
1 kg eggplants
1 cup grated mild cheddar cheese
1 cup cream
half a cup olive oil
black pepper
roasted red pepper slices
1 tbsp fresh dill, finely chopped

PREPARATION:

Wash and clean the artichokes. Place them side by side in a large pan. Add salt, sugar, lemon juice and 1–1.5 cups of water. Cook first over a high heat and then turn the heat down until the artichokes become tender.

Fry the onion in olive oil. Then, roast the eggplants, peel them and cut them into small slices. Add the fried onion, grated cheese, cream, lemon juice, a tablespoon of olive oil, salt, and black pepper, and puree in a food processor or blender.

Place the artichokes on a serving dish. Fill with the eggplant puree.

Garnish with roasted red pepper slices and dill before serving.

Note: For the garnish, it is possible to buy canned roasted red peppers.

STUFFED EGGPLANTS
(SERVES 4)

INGREDIENTS

4 eggplants
1 cup flour
1.5 cups water
1 tsp red pepper
4 onions, cut into chunks
4 bell peppers, cut into matchsticks
2 cloves garlic, crushed
4 red peppers, sliced
1 tsp olive oil
half a bunch of parsley, finely chopped
half a bunch of fresh dill, finely chopped
salt

PREPARATION:

Peel the eggplants. Cut in them half lengthwise and carve out their middle parts to create pockets. Whisk the flour, water, red pepper and a half a teaspoon of salt together to make a batter, which is not very thick. Coat the eggplants in the batter and fry in hot oil.

Fry the onions, peppers, garlic and salt. Fry until the vegetables soak up their own juices. Remove from heat and leave to cool.

Fill the pockets in the fried eggplants with the stuffing. Sprinkle dill and parsley over the dish and serve.

BROAD BEANS WITH YOGURT
(SERVES 2)

INGREDIENTS

10 oz/250 g lamb meat, cut into chunks
half a cup garbanzo beans, soaked overnight
1 lb/500 g fresh broad beans
3–4 cloves garlic, finely chopped
1 tsp black pepper
1 cup yogurt
salt
butter
dried mint

PREPARATION:

Simmer the meat slowly in just enough water to cover it, removing any foam that comes to the surface as it cooks. Add the soaked garbanzo beans and continue to cook.

Cut the broad bean pods into two or three pieces, depending on their size. Once the meat and the garbanzo beans are tender, add the broad beans, garlic and black pepper, and continue to cook.

Whisk the yogurt. Take the pan off the heat and slowly stir the yogurt into the pan with the meat and beans. Add the salt last, to prevent the yogurt from curdling.

Melt the butter with the dried mint and drizzle on top before serving.

ARTICHOKE WITH BROAD BEANS
(SERVES 4)

INGREDIENTS

6 artichoke hearts
juice of half a lemon
1 lb/500 g broad beans, without pods
2 onions, cut into medium chunks
1 cup olive oil
1 tbsp sugar
salt
half a bunch of fresh dill, finely chopped

PREPARATION:

Soak artichokes in water with lemon juice.

Use half of the olive oil to fry the onions. Add the broad beans and one cup of water, bring to the boil, cooking until beans are tender.

Line up the artichokes in a pot. Fill the center of each artichoke with the beans and onions. Sprinkle a dash of salt and sugar on each one, and drizzle the remaining olive oil over them. Add half a cup of hot water and simmer on a low heat or steam until artichokes are tender.

Remove from heat. Allow to cool and garnish with dill before serving.

OLIVE OIL
DISHES

İMAM BAYILDI
(SERVES 4)

INGREDIENTS

4 eggplants
1 cup olive oil
2 onions, sliced
2 bell peppers, chopped
2 cloves garlic, finely chopped
3 tomatoes, skinned and chopped
1 tbsp tomato paste
1 tsp salt
1 tsp sugar
a third of a bunch of parsley, finely chopped
1 tsp of pepper flakes

GARNISH:

slices of green cayenne (or milder) pepper
slices of tomato

PREPARATION:

Peel the eggplants and soak them in salted water. Drain, pat dry with a clean cloth or kitchen paper, and then fry in hot oil. Line the eggplants on an oven tray or ovenproof dish to cool. Fry the onions, peppers and garlic in the olive oil until they are slightly golden, and then add the tomatoes. When the tomatoes are soft, add the tomato paste. Cook for a few more minutes, then add a cup of water and allow to simmer for 10 minutes. Add the salt, sugar, finely chopped parsley and pepper flakes, and stir. Drain any liquid into a cup and reserve.

Slit each eggplant down the middle and push spoonfuls of the cooked mixture into the pockets you have made. Drizzle the reserved sauce over the eggplants. Top with tomato slices and pepper slices.

Cook in the oven at 150 °C (300 °F) for 15 minutes. Allow to cool and serve.

Note: When preparing this or any other stuffed eggplant dish, if you slit the eggplant before frying, the pocket will be easier to make and tidier in appearance.

STUFFED PEPPERS
(SERVES 6)

INGREDIENTS

1.5 cups olive oil
1 tbsp pine nuts
3 cups rice
4 large onions, finely chopped
2 tbsp currants
5 tbsp dried mint
2 tbsp allspice
6 tsp sugar
10–11 large bell peppers
salt to taste

PREPARATION:

Fry the pine nuts and the onions very gently in some of the oil until slightly golden. Add the washed and drained rice. Fry for a few minutes more. Add 6 cups hot water and the other ingredients. Cook over a low heat until the rice has absorbed all the water and is tender.

While the rice is cooking, cut the tops of the peppers and set aside. Remove the seeds from the peppers and make holes in bottom of each with a fork. Stuff the peppers with the rice and onion mix. Put their tops back on and pack them upright in a large saucepan side by side. Add hot water and the rest of the olive oil. Close the lid tightly, bring to the boil and simmer for one hour. Leave to cool and serve cold.

Note: You may cover your peppers with tomato slices if you prefer.

STUFFED VINE LEAVES
(SERVES 2-3)

INGREDIENTS

10 oz/250 g vine leaves
5 onions, diced
1/2 cup olive oil
1 oz/20 g currants
1 oz/20 g pine nuts
1 bunch fresh dill
1 bunch parsley
1 cup rice
black pepper
red pepper flakes

PREPARATION:

Remove the tough outer stem of each vine leaf up to the edge of the leaf. Put the vine leaves in a large saucepan with plenty of water. Bring to the boil and simmer for about 5 minutes. Remove the pan from the heat (boiling is only for fresh leaves, salted ones do not need to be boiled).

Meanwhile, fry the onions in the olive oil until translucent. Add the currants and rice and continue to fry. Just before removing from the heat, add the pine nuts, then the parsley and dill. Leave the mixture to cool.

Lay a vine leaf out flat, put a teaspoon of the rice mixture in the centre, turning in the sides of the leaf; fold them over the mixture and roll up the leaf gently.

Place the vine leaf rolls in layers in a large saucepan. Add enough water to cover the vine leaf rolls, and bring to the boil. When the water begins to boil, drizzle the remaining olive oil over the leaves. Cook on a low heat for 45 minutes.

STUFFED ZUCCHINI WITH DILL
(SERVES 6)

INGREDIENTS

1.5–2 cups olive oil
2 lb/1 kg zucchini
6–7 medium onions, finely chopped
2.5 cups rice
1 tbsp currants
1 tbsp pine nuts
half a bunch of fresh dill, finely chopped
half a bunch of mint, finely chopped
1 tsp allspice
3 tsp sugar

PREPARATION:

Fry the onion and the pine nuts until slightly golden. Add the rice and fry for a few minutes before adding 5 cups of water and the salt. Cook over a medium heat until the rice is still moist and then add the currants. When the currants have puffed up and the rice is ready, turn off the heat and leave to cool, with a closed lid. When the rice has cooled, fluff it once or twice with a fork.

While the rice is cooking and cooling, hollow out the insides of the zucchini, from one end (the other end should remain closed).

Add the chopped mint, dill and other seasonings to the rice and mix well. Stuff the hollowed out vegetables with the rice mixture.

Stack the zucchini in a large saucepan or pot. Place a heat-resistant plate on top of them, add the remaining olive oil and a cup of water and simmer over a low heat until tender, with the lid tightly shut.

FRESH OKRA WITH OLIVE OIL
(SERVES 6)

INGREDIENTS

2 lb/1 kg fresh okra
3–4 onions, chopped
2 cups olive oil
4–5 tomatoes, diced
juice of 1–2 lemons
2 tbsp vinegar
salt

PREPARATION:

Wash the okra well before removing the stems. Drain well and lay out on a kitchen cloth to dry. When dry, pare off the stems, leaving a cone shape around the top of each.

Sauté the diced onions in the olive oil, add the diced tomatoes, and fry until the tomatoes are very tender. Add the okra, then the lemon juice, vinegar and any remaining olive oil. Let the ingredients come to the boil in the juices of the okra (if necessary add some water, less than a cup). Add salt when the okra is close to being done.

Serve cold or warm.

Note: Okra should never be put into water or washed after its stems have been removed, as it discharges a mucus-like liquid. It should not be cooked over a low heat, either–it will release slime.

CABBAGE ROLLS
(SERVES 8)

INGREDIENTS

1 medium cabbage (loose-leafed)
1/2 cup olive oil
1 lb/500 g onions, finely chopped
2 tbsp pine nuts
2.5 cups rice
2 tbsp tomato paste
2 tbsp currants
3 tbsp sugar
salt
1/2 bunch of parsley, finely chopped
1/2 bunch of fresh dill, finely chopped
1/2 bunch of fresh mint leaves, finely chopped
1 tsp allspice
1 tsp cinnamon
juice of 1 lemon
black pepper

PREPARATION:

Separate the cabbage leaves and boil in salted water for 5 minutes. Drain and leave to cool. Fry the onions and pine nuts until golden. Add the rice and fry until the rice turns slightly transparent. Add the tomato paste, currants, sugar and salt. Add enough hot water to cover the mixture and leave on a low heat until the rice is cooked. Remove from the heat, add the parsley, dill, mint, allspice, cinnamon, and lemon juice; mix.

Cut large pieces from the cabbage leaves. Lay them flat and places spoonfuls of the rice mixture in the middle of each leaf. Turn in the sides over the mixture and then roll each leaf up without pressing too hard.

Lay the rolls in rows in a large saucepan, placing any remaining cabbage leaves on top. Add two cups water and any remaining olive oil, and cook on a low heat until the cabbage leaves become soft. (You can drizzle some olive oil over the top for a shinier appearance.)

Cool in pot before moving to a serving dish.

GREEN BEANS WITH OLIVE OIL
(SERVES 5)

INGREDIENTS

2 lb/1 kg green beans (French or runner beans)
1/2 cup olive oil
2 onions, chopped
2 tomatoes, diced
1 tomato, whole
1 tsp sugar
salt

PREPARATION:

Top and tail the beans before cooking.

Fry the onions until slightly golden, then add the diced tomatoes to the pot. Add sugar and salt, mix and remove from the heat. Put the remaining whole tomato into the middle of a large saucepan. Create a ring of beans around it. Add a layer of the onion mix on top of the beans. Create another layer of beans, and another layer of onions, and so on. When all the beans are in the pan, add two cups of hot water.

Cover with a sheet of baking (greaseproof) paper weighed down with a heatproof plate, and close the lid tightly. Simmer until the beans are tender.

Cool in the pan, then turn the beans out, upside down, onto a serving dish.

CELERIAC WITH OLIVE OIL
(SERVES 6)

INGREDIENTS

1 small carrot
2 lb/1 kg medium-sized celeriac
2 handfuls of baby onions, peeled and whole
1/2 cup olive oil
juice of 1 lemon
120 g sweet corn
120 g canned peas
1 bunch of fresh dill, finely chopped
1/2 tsp sugar
salt to taste

PREPARATION:

Cut the carrot into 4 pieces lengthwise, and then slice into 1/2 inch (1 cm) pieces.

Peel the celeriac and cut them into 1/2 inch (1 cm) pieces. Wash, drain and put into a large pan. Lay the baby onions and carrot pieces on top. Add the salt and sugar. Pour the olive oil and enough water to cover the celery roots into the pan, and add a few drops of lemon juice. Cover, bring to the boil, and simmer until tender.

When the celeriac is tender, add the corn and peas, and all the remaining lemon juice. Cook for another 5 minutes.

Drain, turn onto a serving dish, garnish with the dill, and serve.

Note: Beef stock can be used instead of water and olive oil if preferred.

CAULIFLOWER WITH OLIVE OIL
(SERVES 2)

INGREDIENTS

1/4 cauliflower, divided into flowerets
10 baby onions, chopped
3 tbsp olive oil
1 medium carrot, cubed
2 medium potatoes, cubed
1.5 cups warm water
1 tsp vinegar
2 tsp sugar
2 sprigs parsley
2 sprigs fresh dill

PREPARATION:

Fry the baby onions for 5 minutes. Add the diced carrots, then the potatoes and fry for 1–2 minutes more. Add the water and allow to cook for 10 minutes. In a separate pot, simmer the cauliflower in water with salt and vinegar and then add it to the other vegetables. Add the sugar and salt and cook for 10 more minutes. Garnish with dill and parsley after the cauliflower cools.

BORLOTTI BEANS WITH OLIVE OIL
(SERVES 4)

INGREDIENTS

1 cup dry borlotti beans
half a cup of olive oil
1 clove garlic, finely chopped
1 onion, halved and sliced
1 potato, cubed
1 carrot, cubed
1 tbsp tomato paste
2 tsp sugar
salt

GARNISH:

sprigs of parsley
lemon wedges

PREPARATION:

Soak the borlotti beans in water overnight, and drain. Boil in plenty of fresh water until soft, and drain.

Fry the garlic and onion. Add the potatoes and carrots and continue to fry. When they are lightly fried, add the tomato paste and stir. Add the boiled borlotti beans, salt, sugar, and half a cup of boiling water; continue to cook until the water is almost completely absorbed (a little will remain at the bottom).

Allow to cool in the pan and then move to a serving dish. Garnish with parsley and lemon wedges.

RICE AND GRAINS

ALİ PASHA PILAF
(SERVES 6)

INGREDIENTS

2 cups rice
3.5 oz/100 g ground beef
1 onion, grated
1 clove garlic
1/3 cup shelled pistachios
3 tbsp butter
1/2 cup pine nuts
3 cups meat stock
1/3 cup seedless raisins
salt

PREPARATION:

Combine the ground beef, grated onion, garlic, and salt to prepare a meatball mix. Make small, hazelnut-size meatballs, and fry or boil them, as preferred.

Soak the raisins to soften them. Soak the pistachios for 5 minutes and then rub off their skins.

Wash and drain the rice and fry in butter. Add the pine nuts and continue to fry together.

Next, add the meat stock, the meatballs, and the pistachios to the rice. Cook on a low heat for 15–20 minutes, adding the raisins towards the end of the time.

Serve hot.

PEA AND CARROT PILAF
(SERVES 6)

INGREDIENTS

1/3 cup currants
10 oz/250 g of mushrooms
juice of 1 lemon
2 onions, finely chopped
5 tbsp butter
1 tbsp pine nuts
2 cups round rice, rinsed well
2 carrots, grated
5 tbsp canned peas
2–3 sprigs of fresh dill, finely chopped
4 cups meat stock
1 tsp cinnamon
1 tsp sugar
1 tsp black pepper
salt to taste

PREPARATION:

Soak the currants in water until they swell. Boil the mushrooms in water with the lemon juice until tender, then drain, cool, and chop finely.

Fry the onion gently in butter until translucent. Add the pine nuts and rice, and continue to fry. Stir the grated carrot, peas and the drained currants into the rice. Add the meat stock, salt, sugar, cinnamon and black pepper. Cover and cook on a low heat. When the rice is cooked, leave to rest with the lid tightly closed.

Fluff slightly with a fork before serving.

Serve hot.

CHESTNUT PILAF
(SERVES 8)

INGREDIENTS

1 chicken breast
1 chicken leg
1 lb/500 g chestnuts, roasted and peeled
2 carrots, julienned
1 tbsp pine nuts
3 tbsp golden raisins
4 tbsp butter
2 cups rice
4 cups chicken stock
salt
black pepper

PREPARATION:

Soak the rice in salted water for 15 minutes before washing and draining.

Meanwhile, boil the chicken in 4 cups of water, take the meat off the bones, and break into chunks. Place the meat in the bottom of a large saucepan. Scatter the chestnuts and raisins on top.

Fry the pine nuts and carrots in 1 tablespoon of butter, and place them on top of the other ingredients in the saucepan. Add black pepper to taste.

Spread the drained rice on top of the layers of ingredients and pour over the hot chicken stock. Do not stir. Bring to the boil over a high heat, then cook over a low heat until the rice is tender. Melt the rest of the butter and drizzle over the rice.

Turn out upside down onto a dish to serve.

MAKLUBE
(SERVES 10)

INGREDIENTS

2 cups rice
1 lb/500 g lamb (cut into medium-sized chunks)
1/3 cup oil
1 onion, diced
1 kg eggplant, cubed
2 carrots, cubed
4 cups water
salt
black pepper

PREPARATION:

Soak the rice in warm water. While it is soaking, fry the lamb in the oil. Once the juices of the lamb have been reduced, add the diced onion, frying until lightly golden. Place the meat and onion in the bottom of a large saucepan.

Next, fry the eggplants and carrots. Then place them on top of the meat in the pot. Drain the rice and add to the pan in a layer over the other ingredients in the saucepan. Add the water and salt and cook covered on a low heat until the rice has absorbed all the water.

Remove from the heat, turn upside down on to a dish and serve.

Note: This dish looks nice garnished with green lettuce.

MENGEN PILAF
(SERVES 10-12)

INGREDIENTS

1 lb/500 g rice
11 oz/300 g butter
10 oz/250 g onions, finely chopped
1 lb/500 g lamb meat, cut into medium chunks
8 oz/200 g mushrooms, finely chopped
11 oz/300 g tomatoes, skinned and grated
8 cups water
salt to taste
1 tsp sugar
1 bunch of fresh dill, finely chopped
4 oz/100 g walnuts, broken
1 tsp oregano
black pepper

PREPARATION:

Soak in rice salted water for an hour. Wash with cold water and drain.

Meanwhile, fry the finely chopped onions and meat together in a large pan in about half the butter. Once the meat has released its juices, add the mushrooms and tomatoes. Stir gently for a few minutes and then add the water. Bring quickly to the boil and remove any foam that forms on top of the water with a spoon. Turn the heat down and cook on a low heat for half an hour; the meat will be half cooked. Now add the rice, salt and sugar and quickly bring to the boil again. Reduce the heat to low and cook for 15 minutes.

In a separate pan, melt the remaining butter and then pour it over the rice in the large pan. Close the pan lid tightly and remove from the heat. After allowing it to rest for 5–10 minutes, sprinkle with dill, walnuts, oregano and black pepper.

After the pilaf has rested, invert the pan and turn the pilaf out upside down onto a serving dish. Add what is left in the bottom of the pan to the dish. Mix all the ingredients gently with the edge of a bowl, and serve.

Note: The edge of a bowl is used to mix this pilaf to avoid breaking the rice grains, which ruins the dish.

UZBEK PILAF
(SERVES 8)

INGREDIENTS

1 lb/500 g lamb meat, cubed
3 cups short grain rice
3 carrots, julienned
1 tbsp tomato paste
1 onion
3/4 cup sunflower seed oil
1 tsp cumin
1 tsp cinnamon
salt to taste

PREPARATION:

Leave rice to soak in hot, salted water

Fry the finely chopped onions in the oil until translucent. Add the meat and fry until the juices have evaporated. Add the carrots and cook until they become slightly tender. Add the tomato paste and enough water to cover the ingredients. Simmer until the meat is tender.

Drain the rice and add to the pan with the meat and vegetables. Add 3 cups of boiling water, and the salt, cumin and cinnamon. Cook over a high heat until the rice has absorbed all the water. Turn the heat down, and using a spatula form the rice into a dome. This will ensure that the rice cooks evenly. Close the lid tightly and leave the rice to cook very slowly for 20 more minutes.

Finally, turn off the heat, and using a fork, mix the ingredients well. Turn out and serve.

FISH DISHES

SEA BASS STEW
(SERVES 4)

INGREDIENTS

1 sea bass fillet
5 tomatoes
2 green cayenne (or milder) peppers
8 oz/200 g boiled mushrooms
1 onion
4 cloves garlic, finely chopped
1 tbsp oil
1 tbsp butter
2 tbsp mild cheese, grated

PREPARATION:

Cut the fish fillet, tomatoes, peppers, mushrooms, and onion into uniform chunks.

Mix the garlic, oil and salt and place on the bottom of an ovenproof dish. Place the fish and vegetables on top and sprinkle with the cheese. Place the butter on top in the center of the dish. Cook in the oven at 180 °C (350 °F) until the cheese turns a light golden brown (15-10 minutes).

ANCHOVY ROLLS
(SERVES 4)

INGREDIENTS

2 lb/1 kg fresh anchovies
2 tomatoes, finely chopped
2 onions, finely chopped
half a bunch of parsley, finely chopped
1 tsp salt
1 tsp black pepper
1/2 tsp cumin
1/2 cup olive oil
juice of half a lemon

PREPARATION:

Fillet the anchovies and remove their heads. Wash thoroughly and drain.

Mix the tomatoes, onions, parsley, salt, black pepper, and cumin together well. Place spoonfuls of this mix in the center of each anchovy and wrap each one into a roll. Place the rolls on an oven tray and drizzle with the oil and lemon juice.

Bake at 200 °C (390 °F) for 30 minutes, or until the anchovies are cooked, but not dry.

ANCHOVY PILAF
(SERVES 4-6)

INGREDIENTS

2 lb/1 kg fresh anchovies, filleted, heads removed
1 lb/500 g rice
1 large onion, finely chopped
oil
1 tbsp pistachios
1 tbsp currants
salt
pepper
3 cups water

PREPARATION:

Leave rice to stand in salted water for half an hour, then drain.

Fry the onion in oil until golden, then add the drained rice and stir. Add the pistachios, currants, salt, pepper, and 3 cups of hot water. Bring to the boil, cover the pan, and simmer until rice is tender.

Lay half the cleaned anchovies in a large oven dish so that their tails come together at the center. Add half the cooked rice mixture on top, and flatten it into a layer over the anchovies. Make another layer of anchovies and then another layer of rice. Cover with aluminum foil and bake in an oven that has been preheated to 180 °C (350 °F) for 25–30 minutes.

Invert the oven dish and turn out onto a serving dish so that the layer of anchovies is uppermost. Serve.

BONITO WITH BREAD SAUCE
(SINGLE SERVING)

INGREDIENTS

1 bonito fish, cleaned and cut in 2 cm slices
1.5 cups olive oil
1 cup walnuts
1/2 cup flour
1/2 cup vinegar
4–5 large slices dry or stale bread
4 cloves garlic

PREPARATION:

Sprinkle salt on the fish, roll in flour, and fry in olive oil. Remove from pan and place on kitchen paper to remove excess oil. Place on a serving dish.

Remove the bread crusts. Chop the bread in a food processor or blender into it forms breadcrumbs. Soak the breadcrumbs in warm water for a few minutes until they are soft. Drain with a sieve, squeezing them with your hand.

Chop the garlic and walnuts finely in a food processor or blender. Add the breadcrumbs and mix. Add the vinegar and the water, until the sauce has a smooth texture and is of the consistency of yogurt.

Pour over the fish and serve.

STEAMED MACKEREL
(SERVES 2)

INGREDIENTS

2 lb/1 kg mackerel, cleaned
1 onion, cut into rings
half a bunch of parsley, finely chopped
salt
1/3 cup olive oil
1 cup water
juice of 1 lemon
1 sweet bay leaf

PREPARATION:

Line a shallow baking dish with foil. Place onion rings over the base of the dish, followed by the fish. Garnish with the parsley and salt to taste. Leave to stand for about 30–40 minutes.

Pour the olive oil and the water over the fish, add the bay leaf and the lemon juice, and cover with aluminum foil.

Cook in the oven at medium heat for 20–25 minutes (the water will remain).

Serve hot.

FISH SOUP
(SERVES 2)

INGREDIENTS

1 red gurnard, cleaned
5 cups water
1 egg yolk
1 cup mushrooms, boiled and diced
1 medium onion, whole
1/2 tbsp butter
1 tbsp flour
2 celery sticks, sliced finely
3.5 oz /100 g cream or milk
salt
black pepper
3 cloves garlic

PREPARATION:

Boil the red gurnard whole in 5 cups of water. Remove from the pan, reserving the fish stock; remove the skin and cut into small pieces.

Add the potatoes, mushrooms, and onion to the fish stock. Cook until the potatoes and the onion are very tender.

Meanwhile, in a small pan, melt the butter over a gentle heat, add the flour and garlic, and stir constantly with a wooden spoon until the flour begins to brown. Allow to cool and then slowly add some of the fish stock.

In a large pan add the sauce to the fish stock, stirring to avoid lumps. Add the vegetables and fish, celery, cream, salt, and black pepper, and slowly bring to simmering point. Remove from the heat.

Serve hot.

BAKED TROUT
(SERVES 2)

INGREDIENTS

4 trout fillets
8–10 mushrooms, sliced
2–3 green cayenne (or milder) peppers, sliced
1 onion, cut into rings
1 tomato, diced
1 potato, cubed
4 bay leaves
4 tbsp melted butter
greaseproof paper
salt
black pepper

PREPARATION:

Cut two sheets of greaseproof paper in an oval shape large enough to envelop one fish. Place one fillet on each sheet. Put the onion rings, mushrooms, green peppers, potato, salt, black pepper and sweet bay leaves on the fillet. Pour 4 tbsp of butter over the fish. Place the other fillets on top. Fold up the greaseproof paper and cover the fish. Bake in oven at 200 °C (390 °F) for 20–30 minutes and serve.

MEAT DISHES

ÇOBAN KEBAB
(SERVES 2)

INGREDIENTS

1 lb/500 g beef, cut into chunks
2 onions, finely chopped
1 tbsp butter
2 tomatoes, finely chopped
1 cup canned mushrooms, sliced
salt
black pepper
1 tsp red pepper flakes
1 tbsp dried thyme

PREPARATION:

Dry fry the meat. When the meat is cooked, add the mushrooms and butter and continue to fry. When the mushrooms have released their juices, add the onions and cook until they are translucent. Add the tomatoes and reduce the heat. Add the salt and pepper and cook, without a lid, for a few more minutes. Stir with a wooden spoon, season with red pepper flakes and thyme. Serve hot.

Note: Other seasonal vegetables can be added as desired.

ABANOUSH
(SERVES 2)

INGREDIENTS

8 oz/200 g beef, cubed
2–3 bell peppers
3 tomatoes
4 eggplants
3–4 cloves garlic, crushed
2 tbsp butter
salt
black pepper.

PREPARATION:

Cook the peppers, tomatoes, and eggplants under a hot grill until they are tender. Remove the skins and cut into thin slices. Add salt, black pepper, and garlic, and mix well.

Cook the cubed meat in a frying pan with butter until the juices have evaporated. Place the meat on the vegetable mixture prepared and serve.

GROUND LAMB KEBAB
(SERVES 6)

INGREDIENTS

12 tomatoes
2 lb/1kg ground lamb
3 bell peppers, deseeded, cut in strips
salt
black pepper.

PREPARATION:

Thread the tomatoes onto skewers and grill them until the skin begins to blacken. Remove from the skewers, skin the tomatoes, and chop roughly. Lay them on a large tray or serving dish and add salt to taste.

Knead the lamb, salt and black pepper together. Wet your hands and roll meatballs from the mix. Thread the meatballs onto skewers and grill.

When the meatballs are cooked, remove from the skewers and place the meatballs on top of the layer of tomato pieces in the tray.

Scatter the pepper strips over the top. Serve hot with pita bread.

BOSTAN KEBAB
(SERVES 4)

INGREDIENTS

2 eggplants
2 tbsp oil
1 lb/500 g beef, cut in chunks
1 onion, finely chopped
10–12 mushrooms, sliced
3 tomatoes, diced (for stuffing)
1 tomato, sliced (for garnish)
2 bell peppers, diced
salt
black pepper
2 tsp thyme
4 slices mild cheddar cheese
oil

PREPARATION:

Wash the eggplants and peel lengthwise, leaving several strips of skin that run from one end to the other. Carve out a small pocket in the middle of each, cut in half lengthwise, and fry. Put to one side to cool.

Fry the onions until golden, then add the meat, and brown it. Then add the sliced mushrooms and fry all together. When the mushrooms are soft, add the bell peppers and tomatoes and fry until tender. Add salt, black pepper, and thyme, stir and remove from heat. Fill the pockets in the eggplants with this mixture.

Place the stuffed eggplants in an oven dish. Garnish with cheese slices and slices of tomato. Bake at a medium to high temperature until the cheese has slightly melted.

Serve hot.

BEEF WITH BEANS
(SERVES 4)

INGREDIENTS

1 lb/500 g large white beans
8 oz/200 g ground beef
1/2 cup oil
1 tbsp tomato paste
1 tomato
3 bell peppers
1 onion
3–4 cloves garlic
1 tsp salt
5 cups hot water

PREPARATION:

Cover the beans with water and boil for 8–10 minutes.

Fry the onions in oil until slightly golden. Add the meat and fry for 2–3 minutes. Add in the tomatoes which have been cut into chunks, the tomato paste and peppers. Add the beans and water. Cook for 50–55 minutes on low heat. When close to being fully cooked, add salt.

Serve hot.

LAMB STEW WITH ONIONS
(SERVES 4)

INGREDIENTS

1 lb/500 g lamb, cut in chunks
1 lb/500 g baby onions, peeled, washed and left whole
2 tbsp butter
2 tbsp tomato paste
1 tbsp red pepper paste
salt

PREPARATION:

Fry the meat until it has released its juices. Add the baby onions and continue to cook for another 10 minutes. Add the tomato paste, red pepper paste, and salt, and stir until the pan comes to the boil. Add a cup of hot water and cook on a high heat until the meat and onions are tender and the ingredients start to reabsorb their juices.

Remove from heat and serve.

Note: You may substitute olive oil for the butter if you prefer. Half a cup of boiled garbanzo beans can be added with the tomato paste and red pepper paste.

LAMB NECK KEBAB
(SERVES 6-8)

INGREDIENTS

1 lamb neck, jointed
1 onion, whole
3 potatoes, sliced
3 carrots, sliced
1 cup peas
1 bay leaf
juice of 1 lemon
1 egg yolk
half a bunch of parsley, finely chopped
salt

PREPARATION:

Cook the lamb neck in a pressure cooker with the onion and 2 cups water for 15 minutes. When the lamb is cooked, place the potatoes, carrots, peas and bay leaf on top, close the pressure cooker and cook until the potatoes are tender.

Whisk lemon juice and egg yolk together, and then add some of the juices from the meat dish, mixing well. Stir this sauce into the dish, simmer for 2–3 minutes, and then remove from the heat. Add salt to taste.

Turn out onto a serving dish and remove the whole onion and the bay leaf. Garnish with the parsley and serve.

Note: As a final stage, you may place the kebab in an ovenproof dish, grate some mild cheese over the top and bake until the cheese browns before serving.

CHICKEN CREPES
(SERVES 8)

INGREDIENTS

FOR FILLING:
1 large onion, sliced
2 tbsp butter
1 lb/500 g chicken breast, diced
1 tbsp tomato paste
1 red bell pepper, diced
1 large tomato, diced
1 tsp black pepper
1 cup hot water

FOR CREPE BATTER:
3 eggs
1 cup flour
2/3 cup milk
1 tsp salt
half a bunch of parsley, finely chopped

PREPARATION:

First prepare the filling. Fry the onions in the butter. When they are translucent, add the chicken and fry for a few minutes more. Then add the tomato paste, tomato, bell pepper, salt and black pepper with 1 cup hot water, and cook for 15 minutes until all the liquid has been absorbed. Set aside.

To make the crepes, blend the eggs, flour, milk, and salt. Stir in the finely chopped parsley.

Grease and heat a non-stick pan. Make six crepes with the batter, spreading it thinly and evenly across the base of the hot pan. Flip each crepe to ensure both sides are cooked.

Put spoonfuls of the chicken mix on the side of each crepe and roll it up. Cut the crepes in half and lay in an oven dish. Bake at medium heat for 10 minutes, and serve hot.

EGGPLANT KEBAB
(SERVES 4)

INGREDIENTS

2 lb/1 kg eggplants
1 lb/500 g ground beef
1 tsp cumin
1 tsp black pepper
1 onion
2 cloves garlic, crushed
1/2 bunch parsley, finely chopped
1 cup bread crumbs
1 egg, beaten
4 cups yogurt
1/3 cup oil
1 tsp red pepper

PREPARATION:

First, peel the eggplants without cutting off their stems and grill or roast them. Pour the lemon juice over them to stop them turning brown.

Add all the remaining ingredients, including the oil, to the ground beef. Knead well and break into as many pieces as you have eggplants. Remove the eggplants from the lemon juice and pat dry with kitchen paper. Wrap the eggplants with the meat mixture so that it covers them up to their stems.

Lay the meatball in an oven dish and bake at 180 °C (350 °F) until the tops are browned. Serve hot.

MUSHROOM STEW
(SERVES 6-8)

INGREDIENTS

2 lb/1 kg beef, cut in chunks
10–12 mushrooms, sliced
10–12 baby onions, whole
2 carrots, sliced
1 tsp thyme
2 bay leaves
salt
2 tbsp cornstarch
2 cups milk
1 egg yolk
juice of one lemon
a few sprigs of fresh dill, finely chopped

PREPARATION:

Cook the meat in 3–4 cups of water until tender. Reserve one cup of the stock. Add the vegetables to the meat with the thyme, bay leaf and salt. Cook until the vegetables are tender.

Blend the cornstarch with the reserved cup of meat stock. Add the milk. Stir this mixture into the pan with the meat, stirring constantly until it begins to boil. Simmer for 10 minutes. Once the stew has thickened, remove the pan from the heat, and take out a cupful of the liquid. Add the liquid slowly to the egg yolk and lemon juice mixture, and stir. Gradually stir this mixture back into the stew. Bring to the boil twice and remove from the heat.

Sprinkle with the dill and serve.

YÖRÜK KEBAB
(SERVES 4)

INGREDIENTS

10 oz/250 g lamb, cubed
2 bell peppers, finely chopped
1 tomato, finely chopped
2 onions, finely chopped
5 mushrooms, sliced
3 tbsp oil
1 tbsp lemon juice
5 artichoke hearts
1/2 bunch fresh dill, finely chopped
2 tbsp grated mild cheddar cheese
salt
black pepper

PREPARATION:

Fry the meat, bell peppers, and the onions together until the meat begins to reabsorb its own juices. Add the tomato and mushrooms and fry for another 2 minutes. Add a cup of hot water and bring to the boil. Add salt and black pepper, lower the heat, cover and simmer for half an hour.

Fill a large pan with water, add the lemon juice and bring to the boil. Put the artichoke hearts in the boiling water and cover. Lower the heat and cook for 20 minutes until the hearts are tender. Drain them and place in an oven dish.

Fill the artichoke hearts with the meat stuffing. Mix the dill and grated cheese together and sprinkle over the artichokes.

Bake at 200 °C (390 °F) for 30 minutes, and serve hot.

LAMB WITH SEASONED RICE
(SERVES 4)

INGREDIENTS

2 lb/1 kg lamb, cubed
6 tbsp butter
2 cups rice
1/2 cup pine nuts
1 onion, chopped
1 lamb liver, finely sliced
1/3 cup currants
3 cups meat stock
salt
black pepper
1/2 tsp cinnamon
1/2 tsp allspice
half a bunch of fresh dill, finely chopped

PREPARATION:

Boil the cubed lamb in plenty of water. Remove any foam which forms on the surface of the water. When the meat is tender, drain and place on an oven tray. Roast and turn so both sides are browned.

Meanwhile, melt the butter, and fry the pine nuts and onion until they are golden and the onion is translucent. Add the finely sliced liver and fry. Add the currants, meat stock, salt and spices and boil. Add the rice. Cover and cook until the rice is tender. Allow to stand covered for 20 minutes.

Fluff the rice with a fork. Remove the meat from the oven. Place the meat on a serving dish and surround it with the rice. Garnish with dill.

Serve hot.

FRIED LIVER
(SERVES 4)

INGREDIENTS

1 lb/500 g calf liver, finely chopped
4 onions, diced
4 bell peppers, diced
4 tomatoes, diced
1 green onion, sliced
half a cup of sunflower oil
salt
pepper
1 bunch of parsley, finely chopped

PREPARATION:

Fry the onions in the sunflower oil. Add the bell peppers, liver, tomatoes and green onions, in that order, and continue to fry until the liver is cooked and the vegetables tender. Finally, add the seasoning and parsley. Serve.

STEWED LAMB
(SERVES 4)

INGREDIENTS

1 lb/500 g of lamb, cut in chunks
2 tbsp butter
1 onion, finely chopped
2 green cayenne (or milder) peppers, finely chopped
2 cups orzo pasta
1 cup vermicelli noodles
2 tbsp tomato paste
4 cups hot water
salt
pepper
1 sprig of fresh dill, finely chopped

PREPARATION:

Fry the meat, onion, and green peppers in half of the butter. Mix the tomato paste with a little water and add to the pan. Add salt and pepper and remove from the heat after the juices have evaporated.

In another pan, fry the orzo pasta gently in the remaining butter. Add the meat mixture and stir. Add the hot water and cook on a medium heat until the meat is tender. Stir with a wooden spoon and divide between serving dishes.

Garnish with dill and serve.

KARNIYARIK
(SERVES 4)

INGREDIENTS

4 eggplant
1/2 pound ground beef (250 g)
2 tomatoes, slice
1 onion, finely chopped
4 green cayenne (or milder) peppers
1.5 cup water
red pepper flakes
salt
oil for frying

PREPARATION:

Peel the eggplants in strips (leave an inch strip of skin between the peeled parts to ensure the eggplant does not fall apart when frying). Slice the eggplants down the center (but not all the way through) and place in salted water for about 10 minutes. Remove and dry with kitchen towels and fry in the oil, so that they are uniformly browned, and cooked through.

While you are frying the eggplants, fry the onion in a little oil. Add the ground beef, and brown it. Add pepper and salt.

Place the eggplants in an ovenproof casserole, and lightly salt the inside of the eggplants. Place the meat filling inside and put a slice of tomato and a pepper on top of each one. Pour the water over the eggplants and place in the oven (or, if one prefers, this could all be done in a frying pan on the stovetop). Bake at 350 °F, 180 °C for about 1/2 hour, until the tomatoes and peppers are cooked.

PASTRIES

BOSNIAN PASTRY
(SERVES 8)

INGREDIENTS

2 lb/1kg all-purpose flour
3 onions, diced
3 large potatoes, diced into very small pieces
1 cup oil
1 tbsp butter
salt black pepper

PREPARATION:

Mix the flour with salt and enough water to form a dough. Knead until it does not stick to your hand and leave to stand for 1 hour.

Mix the potatoes and onions with salt and black pepper.

Separate the dough into 8 balls. Dust them with flour and roll into rounds that are as thin as you can make them. Drizzle some oil on each round of dough and fold it in half.

Place the potato stuffing along the fold of the pastry. Fold the opposite edge over the potato mixture. Holding the pastry from both ends, gather it towards the middle, making accordion folds.

Place the pastry in the center of a pre-greased round tray, and wrap it around itself. Continue to place the other pastries around the first one until the tray is filled from the center out. Bake for about 30 minutes at 180 °C (350 °F).

Boil 1 cup of water and the butter; pour this (gently) over the pastry. Place in the oven once again and bake for 5 minutes.

Note: As a final stage, you may place the kebab in an ovenproof dish, grate some mild cheese over the top and bake until the cheese browns before serving.

HUNTER'S PASTRY
(SERVES 8)

INGREDIENTS

FILLING:

12 oz/300 g ground beef
2 medium onions
salt and pepper
2 tbsp oil

CREPES:

4 eggs
2 cups milk
1.5 cups all-purpose flour
1 tsp salt
2 tbsp melted margarine

COATING:

1/2 cup all-purpose flour
2 eggs, beaten
1 cup dry breadcrumbs

PREPARATION:

First make the filling. Fry the onions until translucent, then add the ground beef, salt and pepper, and fry some more.

Place the ingredients for the crepes in a mixer and blend until mixture is smooth. Grease a non-stick frying pan lightly. Pour enough crepe mix into the pan to spread it thinly across the base. Cook each side until golden (about 3 minutes). Repeat until you have used all the batter for the crepes.

Fill the crepes with the beef mixture and roll them up. Brush beaten egg along the outer edge of the crepe rolls and press together lightly so the filling does not come out. Roll the filled crepes first in the flour, then in the eggs and then in breadcrumbs and fry. When they are golden, take out of the oil and stand on kitchen paper to remove excess oil.

Serve hot.

PASTRY ROLLS WITH MEAT FILLING
(SERVES 8)

INGREDIENTS

FILLING:

2 lb/1 kg ground lamb
4 tbsp oil
4 onions, roughly chopped
1/2 bunch parsley, finely chopped
salt and pepper

GARNISH:

1 cup yogurt,
red pepper flakes
3 tbsp butter

PASTRY:

3 or 4 ready-made filo pastry sheets
1 cup oil for frying

PREPARATION:

Cook the lamb in one tablespoon of oil on low heat until it releases its juices and these are evaporated. Add the onions, salt, and black pepper and mix. Cook until onions are soft, remove from heat, and drain any fat. Add the parsley and stir.

Place a damp towel over the pastry sheets that are not being used to prevent them drying out. Divide each pastry sheet into about 8 triangles, about 5 inches in length, and 5 inches at the widest part. Place a teaspoonful of the meat mix on each triangle. Brush the edges with water, fold in over the filling, and roll the rectangle up into a cigar shape.

Fry each of the pastry rolls in sizzling oil.

Whisk the yogurt with a little water until it is the consistency of pouring cream. Fry the red pepper flakes in the butter.

Place the pastries on a serving dish and drizzle with the yogurt and then the butter and pepper flakes. Serve hot.

SPINACH WRAPS
(SERVES 8)

INGREDIENTS

500 g spinach,
2 green onions, sliced finely
1 sujuk sausage, finely chopped (see note)
3 tbsp sugar
1 cup oil
1 cup yogurt
1 tbsp vinegar
2–3 cups all-purpose flour
1 tsp baking soda
1 tsp salt
2 tbsp oil (in the spinach)
1 cup of grated mild cheese

PREPARATION:

Fry the spinach leaves in two tablespoons of oil with the green onions. When the water from the leaves has evaporated, add the chopped sausage and mix. Add salt and 1 teaspoon of sugar, and remove from the heat. Add the grated cheese and stir. Set aside to cool while you make the pastry.

Mix 1 cup of oil with the yogurt, vinegar, salt and baking soda and work in enough flour to make a soft dough. Cover the dough and leave to stand for half an hour.

Divide the dough into two and roll out into two large rectangles (the dough should be very thin). Spread half of the spinach filling evenly over one of the rectangles of dough. Place the other rectangle of dough on top of this layer of filling. Make another layer with the remaining spinach filling and then roll the pastry up into a long stick (like a Swiss Roll). Now cut into 2-inch (5cm) slices.

Place the slices on a lined, greased baking tray, brush with egg yolk, and bake at 180 °C (350 °F) until golden.

Note: Sujuk is a hard, spicy, Turkish sausage, made with beef, garlic and cumin. If you cannot buy it another similar sausage can be substituted.

KANDİL RINGS
(SERVES 6)

INGREDIENTS
6 oz/150 g margarine
4 cups all-purpose flour
1 egg, beaten
1 oz/20 g yeast
half a cup warm water
1 tsp. sugar
1 tbsp mahaleb (see note)
1 tsp salt.

GLAZE:
1 egg yolk, beaten
1 cup sesame seeds
black cumin seeds

PREPARATION:
Mix the yeast with the warm water and sugar. Allow to stand for 10 minutes. Sift the flour in a mixing bowl and make a well in the centre. Melt the margarine, allow to cool slightly. Pour the margarine, yeast mixture, 1 beaten egg, the mahaleb and salt into the well in the centre of the flour, and knead. Cover the dough with a moist cloth and leave to rise in a warm place for 25–30 minutes.

Break egg-sized pieces from the dough. Roll into cylinders as thick as your finger. Join the ends to create rings. Lay the rings on a greased tray, glaze them with the egg yolk, and sprinkle half of them with sesame seeds and half with black cumin seeds.

Bake for 20 minutes in an oven pre-heated to 180 °C. Serve with tea or coffee.

Note: Mahaleb (or mahlep) is the seeds of a small Eurasian ornamental tree (Prunus mahaleb), used in Middle Eastern cooking, available from specialist shops.

SPLIT PASTRY WITH MEAT
(SERVES 6)

INGREDIENTS

3 filo pastry sheets

FILLING:

12 oz/300 g ground beef
2 onions, finely chopped
1 tbsp margarine
2 tbsp dried breadcrumbs
1 cup oil
1 cup water
salt and pepper
2 tomatoes, sliced
2 peppers, sliced

PREPARATION:

Fry onions and ground beef in the margarine. Add salt and pepper to taste.

Whisk the water and the oil together. Lay out the pastry sheets on a flat surface and brush with the water and oil mixture. Fold each sheet over and brush with the mixture again. Cut across each sheet diagonally so you have 6 triangles.

Place spoonfuls of the ground beef filling at the wider end of each triangle and roll it up into a baton. Dip the baton into water and then roll in the breadcrumbs. Place the batons on a greased baking tray and slit lengthwise with a sharp knife.

Garnish each baton with a tomato and pepper slice and bake in oven at 180 °C (350 °F) until golden.

SPINACH PASTRY ROLLS
(SERVES 8)

INGREDIENTS

PASTRY:

5 cups all-purpose flour
3 eggs
1 cup cold water
salt
4 oz/100 g margarine
1 egg yolk

FILLING:

1 lb/500 g spinach
1 large onion, finely chopped
1/2 bunch of fresh dill, finely chopped
3 tsp dried mint
10 oz/250 g cheese, grated
black pepper
poppy seeds (optional)

PREPARATION:

Mix the flour, 3 eggs, water and salt together, kneading until the dough is elastic and does not stick to your hands. Cover the dough and leave to wait for half an hour.

Wash and chop the spinach. Fry the onion, remove from the heat and add the spinach, dill, mint, cheese, salt and black pepper and mix.

Break off fist-sized pieces of the dough and roll out into circles until they measure 12" in diameter (30–40 cm) (they will be very thin). Melt the margarine and brush the pastry circles with this. Spread the filling on each pastry circle, leaving about 3" (7–8cm) empty along the edge. Fold the two opposite sides to meet in the middle and roll up loosely to form a baton shape.

Place the pastries on a greased and lined round baking tray; start from the center and roll the pastry round itself. Continue to place the pastries round the center one, so the tray fills up from the center out.

Brush with the egg yolk and water and bake at 250 °C (480 °F) until crispy. Cut into slices before serving.

Note: The pastry can be sprinkled with poppy seeds before baking.

LAHMAJUN
(MAKES 6)

INGREDIENTS

6 cups all-purpose flour
1/2 oz dry yeast
1 cup warm water
1 tsp sugar
1 tsp salt

TOPPING:

12 oz/300 g ground beef
1 large tomato, finely chopped
1 large onion, finely chopped
1 tsp black pepper
1 tsp cumin
1 tbsp red pepper paste
1 tbsp tomato paste
half a bunch of parsley, finely chopped
1 tsp red pepper flakes
2 tbsp oil

PREPARATION:

Mix the yeast, warm water and sugar, and leave to stand until froth forms. Sift the flour and make a well in the middle. Add the yeast mixture to the flour, add salt and knead with enough water to form a soft dough. Cover and leave dough in a warm place to rise for an hour.

Meanwhile, prepare the topping. Mix the ground beef, oil, tomatoes, onions, black pepper, cumin, red pepper paste, tomato paste, salt, parsley, and red pepper flakes, and knead with enough water to give a slightly mushy mixture.

Break the risen dough into six pieces. Roll into balls and roll out into large flat circles. Spread the topping thinly on the dough circles. Bake in an oven preheated to 180 °C (350 °F).

Note: Serve with red onions, sumac and parsley.

MANTI (TURKISH RAVIOLI)
(SERVES 8)

INGREDIENTS
DOUGH:
4 cups all-purpose flour
3 eggs
1 tbsp salt
1 cup water
4 cups beef stock

FILLING:
1 lb/500 g finely ground beef
2 onions, finely chopped
salt and pepper

SAUCE:
4 cups yogurt
2–3 cloves garlic, crushed
3 tbsp butter
1 tsp red pepper flakes
1/2 tsp salt

PREPARATION:

Knead the flour, egg, salt, and water together to make a smooth dough. Divide the dough into fairly large pieces (size of a grapefruit) and roll into very thin sheets (1 mm thick). Cut into 1" (3cm) squares.

Meanwhile, mix the ground beef, onions, salt and black pepper for the filling. Place a tiny quantity of this stuffing in the center of each square of dough. Pinch the four corners of each square together to create a small bundle.

Place the bundles on a greased and lined baking tray and bake at 200 °C (390 °F) until they are a light golden color.

Now bring the 4 cups of beef stock to a boil in a large pan, add the bundles, and cook for 5–6 minutes. Drain.

Whisk the yogurt with the garlic, and pour over the bundles. Finally, melt the butter, salt and the red pepper flakes, pour this over the top of the bundles, and serve.

CHEESE PASTRY (SU BÖREĞİ)
(SERVES 8)

INGREDIENTS

1 lb/500 g all-purpose flour
5 eggs, beaten
1 cup oil
10 oz/250 g margarine, melted
1/2 bunch parsley, finely chopped
12 oz/300 g feta cheese, crumbled
salt
some starch and flour.

PREPARATION:

Sift the flour and salt, and work in the eggs and enough warm water to create a dough that is not sticky but is easy to work. Divide the dough into 12 balls. Cover with a damp cloth and allow to rest for 15 minutes. Roll out each ball into a sheet that is 3–4 millimeter thick.

Fill a large pan with water, add salt and the cup of oil, and bring to the boil. When the water is boiling, put pastry sheets in the pan and boil for 2–3 minutes. To make sure they do not stick together, you may need to boil only two at a time. After boiling for 2–3 minutes, take the sheets out of the pan and place in cold water.

Take the sheets out of the cold water and pat dry with a clean cloth. Lay a sheet of pastry on a greased baking tray, and brush with melted margarine. Sprinkle lightly with cheese and parsley. Lay another sheet of pastry over the cheese layer, brush with margarine, sprinkle with cheese and parsley, and continue until you finish all the pastry sheets.

Brush margarine over the top and bake at 180 °C (350 °F) until golden on top. Cut into large squares and serve.

Note: If you put 1–2 lumps of citric acid into the hot water you are using for the pastry, your pastry sheets will not shred.

CHEESE AND OLIVE BREAD
(SERVES 8)

INGREDIENTS

3 eggs
1 cup milk
3/4 cup oil
2 cups all-purpose flour
1 cup cheese (feta or other mild cheese), grated
1/2 bunch fresh dill, chopped
10–15 green olives, pitted and cut into rings
1 tsp baking powder

PREPARATION:

Whisk the eggs with the milk and oil. Fold in the baking powder and flour.

Reserve about a third of the olive rings. Mix the remainder with the dill and cheese and stir into the bread mix.

Pour the mix into a greased cake mould. Decorate the top with the remaining olive rings. Bake at 160 °C (320 °F) for 40–50 minutes.

VEGETABLE MUSKA
(SERVES 3)

INGREDIENTS

FILLING:

1 large leek, finely chopped
1 medium carrot, finely chopped
1 medium celeriac or 2 pieces of celery, finely chopped
10 oz/250 g ground beef
1 onion
3 tbsp butter

PASTRY:

3 filo pastry sheets
3 tbsp olive oil
1 egg yolk
1 tsp cumin seeds
2–3 tsps sesame seeds

PREPARATION:

Fry the leek, carrot, and celery or celeriac over a low heat in a tablespoon of butter. Next, fry the ground beef and onion in a dry pan, with salt and black pepper. When the beef is cooked, add the vegetables and stir.

Brush the pastry sheets with oil and cut into wide strips. Place the filling on one end of the pastry strips and fold the end closest to you to the right edge, over the filling, to make a small triangle. Continue folding the triangle over itself until the end of the strip. Brush with the egg yolk and sprinkle with black cumin seeds and sesame seeds. Bake at 350 °F until golden brown.

GROUND BEEF PASTRY
(SERVES 8)

INGREDIENTS

8 cups all-purpose flour
6 eggs, beaten
10 oz/250 g margarine
1 tsp salt
water

FILLING:

2 oz/50 g margarine
1 lb/500 g ground beef
1 medium onion, finely chopped
1/2 bunch of parsley, finely chopped
1/3 cup melted margarine
salt

PREPARATION:

Work the flour, eggs, margarine and salt with enough water to make a soft, elastic dough. Break into 8 pieces. Cover with a damp cloth and leave to rest for 15–20 minutes.

Meanwhile, make the filling. Fry the onion in 2 ounces of margarine until transparent. Add the ground beef and fry until the juices have evaporated. Add the salt, black pepper, and parsley, stir and remove from the heat.

Bring a large pan of water to the boil. Add 1 tablespoon of salt and 2 tablespoons of oil. Roll out the 8 pieces of dough into very thin sheets. Boil them, one by one, in the salted water for 1–2 minutes. Then dip into cold water. Pat dry with a kitchen cloth.

Using 4 sheets of dough and half of the filling, spread the first sheet over a greased and lined round baking tray (or large non-stick frying pan). Brush with the melted margarine. Place the ground beef filling on top, then another sheet of pastry, a layer of beef and a layer of pastry until you have four layers of pastry and three layers of filling. Repeat these steps with the remainders of the ingredients.

Fry the pastry on one side, until golden. Flip out onto a plate, and invert the plate to fry the other side of the pastry. Cut into squares and serve warm.

CANDIED FRUIT CAKE
(SERVES 8)

INGREDIENTS

4 eggs
1.5 cups sugar
1 cup yogurt
5 oz/125 g margarine, melted
3 cups all-purpose flour
1 tsp vanilla essence
1 tsp baking powder
1 cup mixed candied fruit
zest of one lemon
1/4 cup chocolate chips
1/4 cup raisins

PREPARATION:

Whisk the eggs and sugar for about 8–10 minutes, until light and fluffy. Fold in the yogurt, margarine and vanilla essence. Sift the flour and baking powder together and fold into the mixture.

Add the candied fruits, lemon zest, chocolate chips and raisins, and mix so that they are evenly distributed throughout.

Bake at 170 °C (340 °F) for 40–45 minutes. Allow to cool and slice before serving.

Note: This cake can be made with chopped dried fruit, such as figs, apricots, and raisins, or sliced fresh fruit like apples and oranges. To ensure the dried fruit does not sink to the bottom of the cake, you can boil it in 1 cup of water for 5–6 minutes before mixing into the dough.

TAHINI SWIRLS
(SERVES 8-10)

INGREDIENTS

5 cups all-purpose flour
1 tbsp yeast
1/2 cup milk
1 cup oil
1 egg, beaten
1 tsp salt
1 tsp sugar

FILLING:

1 cup tahini,
1 cup sugar,
1/2 cup walnuts, broken into large pieces

PREPARATION:

Mix the yeast with the warm milk and a teaspoon of sugar. Leave aside until it is frothing. Sift the flour and salt into a large bowl, and make a well in the centre. Pour in the yeast, oil, and egg and mix to make a dough. Cover and leave to rise in a warm place until the dough doubles in size.

Knead the dough, and divide into three equal pieces. Roll out each piece into a rectangular sheet a quarter of an inch (half a centimeter) thick.

Now brush plenty of tahini over the first pastry sheet and sprinkle with sugar. Place another sheet of pastry on top and then more tahini and sugar. Repeat with the third sheet. Scatter crushed walnuts on top and then roll up the layers of dough.

Cut slices across the roll. Place them on a greased and lined oven tray. Bake at medium heat until the pastries are light gold in color.

Note: You may make tahini swirls without sugar as a savory pastry.

POPPY SEED COOKIES
(SERVES 8-10)

INGREDIENTS

slightly less than one cup confectioner's sugar
8 oz/200 g margarine
2 eggs
2 tsp lemon zest
4 dried cloves, crushed
4 cups all-purpose flour
1 tsp baking powder
1/2 cup poppy seeds, crushed
1/2 cup sugar
confectioner's sugar to dust

PREPARATION:

Cream the sugar and margarine together at room temperature until light and fluffy. Fold in the eggs, lemon zest, and cloves, and continue to mix for 10–15 minutes. Sift the flour and baking powder together and fold into the mix to make a dough.

Roll the dough out on aluminum foil to form a rectangle a quarter of an inch (half a centimeter) thick. Sprinkle the poppy seeds over the rectangle and then roll up the dough. Cut into slices about half and inch (1 centimeter) thick.

Put the slices on a greased and lined baking tray. Bake at 190 °C (375 °F) for 15 minutes. Dust with confectioner's sugar before serving.

HAZELNUT COOKIES
(SERVES 4)

INGREDIENTS

3 cups ground hazelnuts
just under 1 cup confectioner's sugar
3 tbsp all-purpose flour
1 egg, beaten
5 oz/125 g margarine, melted
15–20 large hazelnut, broken

PREPARATION:

Combine the hazelnuts, sugar, flour, egg, and margarine to make a dough. Divide into small walnut-sized balls. Top with broken hazelnuts.

Bake at 200 °C (390 °F) for 10–15 minutes until slightly golden.

PRALINE CAKE
(SERVES 4)

INGREDIENTS

PRALINE:

1 tbsp pistachios, roughly chopped
1 tbsp skinned almonds
4 tbsp sugar
1 tbsp water
1 tbsp margarine, melted

CAKE:

5 eggs
6 tbsp sugar
5 tbsp all-purpose flour
4 tbsp cocoa
1/2 tsp baking powder
1 tbsp margarine, melted

SAUCE:

80 g chocolate, melted

PREPARATION:

Heat 1 tablespoon of margarine in a pan; 4 tablespoons of sugar in the melted margarine. Add the pistachios and almonds and fry until slightly golden. While still hot, spread this mixture thinly over a greased baking sheet, and leave to cool.

While the praline is cooling, beat the eggs and 6 tablespoons of sugar for 8–10 minutes, until very light and frothy. Sift the flour, baking powder, and cocoa, and then fold gently into the egg and sugar mix with a spatula.

Break the cooled praline into small pieces. Fold the other tablespoon of margarine and half of the broken praline into the dough and mix well so the praline is evenly distributed throughout.

Bake at 160 °C (320 °F) for 35 minutes. Remove from the oven and allow to cool.

Pour the melted chocolate (by the bain-marie method) over the cake and sprinkle with remaining praline before serving.

CORN FLOUR CAKE
(SERVES 6)

INGREDIENTS

1.5 cups sugar
3 eggs
1 cup milk
1 cup yogurt
3/4 cup oil
1 tsp baking soda
1 tsp cinnamon
half a cup all-purpose flour
3 cups corn flour
1 cup walnuts, broken
half a cup sesame seeds

PREPARATION:

Beat the sugar and eggs together for 10 minutes in a food processor. Add the milk, yogurt, and oil, and beat. Sift the baking soda, cinnamon, flour and corn flour together. Add this to the food processor and mix. Fold in the walnuts and pour the dough into a cake mould. Sprinkle sesame seeds on top and bake at 170 °C (340 °F) for 40 minutes.

DESSERTS

BAKLAVA
(SERVES 10)

INGREDIENTS

1 packet filo pastry
1/2 pound (250 g) butter
1.5 cup walnuts (or pistachio nuts)

SYRUP:

3.5 cups water
3.5 cups sugar
juice from half a lemon

PREPARATION:

Place two sheets of filo pastry on shallow baking dish (12 x 8 or larger). Generously paint with melted butter then place on another sheet of filo. Paint this with the butter as well. Continue in this way until half the packet has been used up, and then sprinkle on the walnuts. Then continue to place the filo pastry, generously buttering each layer. With a sharp knife, cut through the layers and then brush, once again, very generously with the melted butter. Cook in an oven preheated to 170 °C (340 °F) and bake for about 35-40 minutes. Take out of the oven and make the syrup by putting the water, sugar and lemon juice into a pan. Bring these to the boil, stirring to make sure the mixture does not caramelize. While the syrup is still warm it should be poured over the cooled baklava with a ladle, slowly, giving time for the syrup to be absorbed.

KADAYIF WITH WALNUTS
(SERVES 4)

INGREDIENTS

1 pastry sheet
8 oz/200 g kadayıf (see note)
2 oz/50 g melted butter
3.5 oz/100 g walnuts, crushed
2 cups water
2 cups sugar

PREPARATION:

Spread the pastry sheet out flat. Brush with melted butter.

Tease the kadayif so that all the strands are separated; pour the melted butter over the kadayif and work it in, breaking up the strands into small pieces. Spread this mixture over the pastry sheet. Sprinkle a layer of crushed walnuts on top.

Now roll the pastry sheet up. Cut the roll into rings. Place the rings on a greased and lined baking tray and bake in an oven preheated to 180 °C, 360 °F. until golden in color (about 20 minutes).

While the pastry is baking, make a syrup from the water and sugar. Do not allow the syrup to caramelize. Allow to cool.

Pour the syrup over the rings before serving.

Note: Kadayif is a shredded pastry. It can be bought in specialist stores or over the internet.

SWEET RINGS
(SERVES 6)

INGREDIENTS

26 oz/750 g all-purpose flour
2 oz/50 g semolina
1 tbsp. yeast
1 tsp baking powder
1 tbsp lemon juice
4.5 pints/2 liters oil to fry

SYRUP:

2 lb/1kg sugar
2.5 cups water

PREPARATION:

Mix the yeast with half a cup of warm water and a teaspoon of sugar; leave until bubbles form. Sift the flour, semolina and baking powder together, and make a well in the centre. Pour the yeast mixture into the well and mix, adding enough warm water to form a soft dough. Cover with a damp cloth and leave in a warm place to rise for 1–2 hours.

While the dough is rising, heat the water and dissolve the sugar to form a clear syrup. Leave to cool.

Either cut rings from the risen dough or pipe through a piping bag and deep fry. Pour the syrup over the rings and leave to soak before serving.

KEMAL PASHA
(SERVES 6)

INGREDIENTS

1 cup + 2 tbsp all-purpose flour
1 tsp baking soda
2 eggs
1.5 oz/40 g margarine
6 oz/150 g unsalted feta cheese, crumbled

SYRUP:

2 cups water
1.5 cups confectioner's sugar
1 tbsp lemon juice

PREPARATION:

Boil 2 cups of water, 1.5 cups of confectioner's sugar and lemon juice to make a clear syrup.

Combine the flour, baking powder, eggs, margarine and cheese to make a dough. With floured hands divide the dough up into 18 pieces. Roll into balls and place on a greased and lined baking tray.

Bake for 20 minutes in an oven preheated to 180 °C (350 °F). Remove from the oven and leave to cool.

Allow the dough balls to cool off slightly and then place in a pan with the syrup. Cook in a pan over low heat for 15 minutes. Allow to cool before serving.

Note: You can prepare this dessert weeks in advance if you keep the dough balls in a tightly sealed container after baking them. Simply prepare the syrup right before you serve them.

CORN FLOUR HELVA
(SERVES 6)

INGREDIENTS

2 cups corn flour
1 cup ground hazelnuts
5 oz/125 g butter
2 cups water
1 cup sugar

PREPARATION:

Boil the sugar and water together to make a syrup and leave to cool. Heat the corn flour in a non-stick pan over medium heat for a few minutes, stirring continuously with a wooden spoon. Melt the butter in a separate pan and then add to the corn flour. Cook for 10 minutes more, continuing to stir. Reserve a tablespoonful of the hazelnuts, and stir the rest into the mixture in the pan. Slowly add the syrup mixture, making sure it mixes well with the helva.

Turn the helva into a round-bottomed dish and leave to cool for a few minutes. Invert the bowl and turn the helva onto a serving dish. Garnish with the reserved hazelnuts and serve warm.

VIZIER'S FINGERS
(SERVES 6)

INGREDIENTS

FOR THE SYRUP:

3 cups water
4 cups water
1 tsp lemon juice
oil for frying

DOUGH:

1.5 cups water
1/4 cup butter
1.5 cup all-purpose flour
6 eggs
salt

PREPARATION:

First, prepare a clear syrup by dissolving the sugar in the water and lemon juice. Simmer until it thickens, without allowing to caramelize, and leave to cool.

Bring the water and butter to the boil. Sift the flour and salt and whisk into the water and oil mixture. Cook for about 5 minutes. Spread the cooked flour on a tray to cool. When it is cool, crack the eggs into the mixture and knead to make a dough.

To prevent the dough sticking to your fingers, dip your fingers into oil, then break walnut-sized pieces from the dough and make into oblong shapes.

Fry until golden brown. Place on a serving dish, pour the warm syrup over them and leave to soak up the syrup before serving.

DAMASCUS CAKE
(SERVES 10)

INGREDIENTS

2.5 cups semolina
1 cup yogurt
1 cup sugar
1 tsp vanilla essence
1 tsp baking soda
2 tbsp salted peanuts

SYRUP:

3 cups sugar
3 cups water
1 tbsp lemon juice

PREPARATION:

Mix the semolina, yogurt, vanilla essence and sugar in a bowl. Add baking soda and stir, and pour into a 30cm square tray that has been brushed with water. Scatter the salted peanuts on top and bake in an oven preheated to 200 °C (390 °F) until golden brown on top.

While the cake is baking, dissolve the sugar in the water and lemon juice. Bring the syrup to the boil. Take the cake out when golden brown and it springs back, and immediately pour the syrup over the cake.

ŞEKERPARE
(SERVES 10)

INGREDIENTS

2 eggs
4 cups all-purpose flour
10 oz/250 g margarine, melted
2 tsps baking powder
1 egg yolk
5 oz/150 g almonds or hazelnuts, whole

SYRUP:

3.5 cups sugar
3.5 cups water
2 tsp lemon juice

PREPARATION:

First make the syrup. Dissolve the sugar in the water and lemon juice. Bring the syrup to the boil and leave to cool.

Whisk the eggs thoroughly. Add the margarine, sifted flour, and baking powder. Knead until the dough is smooth and workable.

Break off walnut-sized pieces of dough and place on a lightly greased and lined baking tray. Brush with egg yolk; place one hazelnut or almond firmly on top of each cake, and press down lightly. Bake at 200 °C (390 °F) for 12 minutes.

Pour the syrup over the cakes as soon as you take them out of the oven. Cover the tray for 5–10 minutes until the shekerpare have soaked up all the syrup. Serve.

QUINCE DESSERT
(SERVES 8)

INGREDIENTS

4 quinces, peeled, halved and cored
seeds of the quinces (to provide pectin for the juice)
8 cups water
6 cups sugar
1 apple, grated
4 oz/100 g raisins
cinnamon
cream

PREPARATION:

Poach the quinces in water with 5 cups of sugar with the seeds and cinnamon until the fruit is tender.

Cook the apple, raisins, 1 cup of sugar, and cinnamon on a medium heat. Line the poached quinces up in an oven dish and fill their centers with the apple mix.

Bake at 180 °C (350 °F) for 10–15 minutes. Allow to cool and serve with cream.

ASHURA (NOAH'S PUDDING)
(SERVES 12)

INGREDIENTS

3 cups whole wheat grains or barley
1.5 cups black-eyed peas
1.5 cups cannellini beans
1.5 cups garbanzo beans
8 cups water
4 cups sugar
10–15 dried apricots, sliced
1/4 cup raisins
1/4 cup hazelnuts
1/4 cup rosewater
zest of 1 orange
10 dried figs, finely chopped

GARNISH:

4 tbsp walnuts, crushed
4 tbsp hazelnuts, crushed
4 tbsp pomegranate seeds

PREPARATION:

Soak the wheat, black-eyed peas, garbanzo beans, and cannellini beans overnight. Boil the four types of grain in four separate pans until tender. Remove the skins from the garbanzo peas if any are loose.

Now put all the cooked grains into one pan and add 8 cups of water. Bring to the boil and add the sugar. (The amount can be adjusted to your taste of sugar to taste.) Simmer until the beans begin to taste sweet. Now add the sliced apricots, raisins and hazelnuts. Bring back to the boil and continue to simmer until the apricots are soft. Add the rose water, orange zest, and figs. Cover and cook until the figs are soft. Leave to cool.

Garnish with walnuts, hazelnuts and pomegranate seeds to serve.Garnir avec les noix, les noisettes et les graines de grenade avant de servir.

APPLE CUSTARD
(SERVES 10)

INGREDIENTS

4 apples, peeled and thinly sliced
2 tsps cinnamon
2 cups confectioner's sugar
4.5 cups milk
1 egg yolk
3.5 oz/80 g all-purpose flour
2 oz/50 g cornstarch
2 oz/50 g margarine, melted
1 tsp vanilla essence
salt

PREPARATION:

Sprinkle half a cup of the confectioner's sugar and cinnamon on the apple slices and poach over a low heat for 20 minutes.

Beat the milk and egg yolk with a pinch of salt. Sift the flour and cornstarch together and mix to a smooth paste with a little of the milk and egg mixture. Stir in the remaining milk and egg mixture, and then the margarine and vanilla essence.

Cook over a low heat, stirring constantly until it thickens. Add the rest of the sugar and remove from the heat once the sugar has dissolved.

Place the apple mixture in the base of a serving dish. Pour the custard over the apple mixture and leave to set. Serve when cool.

STUFFED DATES
(SERVES 6)

INGREDIENTS

20 dates
1/3 cup currants
1/3 cup dried apricots
1/3 cup walnuts
1 tbsp tahini
1 tbsp molasses
1 tsp ginger
1 tsp cinnamon
1 cup flaked coconut

PREPARATION:

Chop the raisins and apricots very finely in a food processor. Mix with the walnuts, tahini, molasses, ginger, and cinnamon. Halve the dates lengthwise and remove their pits. Stuff with the filling mixture. Roll the dates in coconut to coat them. Serve.

STUFFED KADAYIF
(SERVES 10)

INGREDIENTS

1 lb/500 g kadayif
12 oz/400 g walnuts
2 tbsp confectioner's sugar
4 eggs
1 cup milk
oil for frying

SYRUP:

2 cups confectioner's sugar
2.5 cups water
1 tbsp lemon juice

PREPARATION:

First make the syrup. Heat the water and sugar together. Add the lemon juice once the liquid has thickened. Bring to the boil and then remove from the heat. Leave to cool.

Take enough kadayif to fill your hand, open it and fill with the walnuts and sugar before closing again.

Beat the eggs with the milk. Coat the pastries in the egg mix and then fry in hot oil until both sides are golden brown.

While the pastries are hot poor the cold syrup over them. Serve immediately.

KAZANDİBİ
(SERVES 8 – 10)

INGREDIENTS

4 cups milk
1.5 cups confectioner's sugar
1/2 cup rice flour
1 tbsp cornstarch
1 tsp vanilla essence
1 tbsp margarine
3 tbsp confectioner's sugar
cinnamon

PREPARATION:

Sift the confectioner's sugar, rice flour and cornstarch together. Place in a pan and work the milk in slowly, stirring constantly. Place the pan over a gentle heat and bring the mixture to the boil. Simmer and continue to stir for about 15 minutes until the mixture begins to bubble and has thickened. Stir in the vanilla essence and remove from the heat.

Grease a rectangular tray with margarine and sprinkle with confectioner's sugar. Pour the cooked mixture into the tray. Bake at medium heat, until the base is slightly burnt.

Once the bottom is burnt, remove from the oven, and place the baking tray into a larger dish which has cold water in it. Allow to wait for 5 minutes. Remove the tray from the water bath and leave to cool in the refrigerator.

When it is cool, cut the pudding into rectangles and roll up with the caramelized side outwards. Serve.

PUMPKIN DESSERT
(SERVES 4)

INGREDIENTS

1.5–2 lb/800 g pumpkin
4 cups confectioners' sugar
4–5 dried cloves
1 cup water
4 tbsp crushed walnuts

PREPARATION:

Peel the pumpkin, removing any green parts, and cut into 2" (5cm) cubes. Sprinkle sugar over the cubes and leave to stand for 4–5 hours.

Place in a large pan with the cloves and 1 cup of water. Simmer over a low heat for 1 hour. Once the pumpkin has become soft, remove from the heat, and leave to cool.

Garnish with crushed walnuts and serve.

Note: You may also garnish with whipped or clotted cream.

COFFEE PUDDING
(SERVES 6)

INGREDIENTS

FOR THE PUDDING:

2 pints/1 liter milk
2 eggs
1 cup all-purpose flour
1.5 cups sugar
3 tsp coffee

GARNISH:

3 tbsp caramelized pictachios

PREPARATION:

Blend all the ingredients, making sure to eliminate any lumps. Put into a large pan. Heat, whisking, until the liquid thickens.

Divide into serving bowls once it cools.

Sprinkle with caramelized pistachios before serving.

LEMON CLOUD
(SERVES 6)

INGREDIENTS

3 large lemons
1 cup milk
150 g whipping cream
1 cup confectioner's sugar
1 pack lemon jelly
2 cups hot water

GARNISH

2 slices of pineapple

PREPARATION:

Whisk the whipped cream. Leave to stand in the fridge for 10 minutes.

Grate the zest of 1 lemon and squeeze the juice of all 3 lemons. Mix with the confectioner's sugar and allow the juice to dissolve the sugar.

Dissolve the lemon jelly in hot water. Leave to cool. When the jelly is completely cool but not set, fold in the refrigerated whipped cream with a spatula. Add the lemon peel and juice and fold in gently. (Do not beat or use an automatic mixer for this process or it will curdle.)

Line a deep container with a layer of cling film and fill with the lemon mixture. Leave to set in the refrigerator for a day or more.

Turn out on to a serving dish and garnish with the pineapple rings before serving.

CHOCOLATE CAKE
(SERVES 8)

INGREDIENTS

1 pack chocolate cake mix
3 tbsp sugar
2 tbsp instant coffee
1.5 cups water
2 tbsp all-purpose flour
4 tbsp sugar
3 egg yolks
2 cups milk
200 g pack cream cheese
2 tbsp cocoa

PREPARATION:

First make a chocolate cake from the commercial cake mix (or from your own recipe if you prefer).

Dissolve 3 tablespoons of sugar and the instant coffee in 1.5 cups of hot water and leave to cool.

Cut the chocolate cake into two layers. Soak both layers in the coffee syrup mix.

Blend the flour, sugar and egg yolks with the milk and bring to the boil. Simmer for five minutes, then remove from the heat, stir in the cream cheese and mix well.

While the cream topping is still warm, place the bottom layer of the chocolate cake on a serving dish. Spread thickly with the cream, top with the other layer of cake, and spread the rest of the cream over the top.

Leave to cool, then refrigerate for at least 4 hours. Sift some cocoa on top before serving.

APPLE CINNAMON DESSERT
(SERVES 4)

INGREDIENTS

2 golden apples
1 tbsp olive oil
2 tbsp butter
1 tbsp brown sugar
2 tsp cinnamon
whipped cream

PREPARATION:

Peel and core the apples and slice each into 8 pieces. Fry the apples in the olive oil and butter over a medium heat for 3–4 minutes until they become soft. When they are tender, add the sugar and cinnamon and continue to cook until soft but not mushy.

Place on a serving dish and pour over the juices from the pan. Garnish with whipped cream or vanilla ice-cream before serving.

SOUR CHERRY PUDDING
(SERVES 4)

INGREDIENTS

2 cans (15 oz) pitted sour cherries
2 cups water
2 cups confectioner's sugar
5 tbsp cornstarch

PREPARATION:

Drain the cherries and set aside 8–12 of them for garnish. Puree the remainder (in a blender or food processor). Put the puree in a pan with the water, cornstarch, and sugar. Cook over medium heat, stirring constantly until the fruit has a pudding-like consistency. Divide into serving dishes and leave to cool.

Garnish with the reserved cherries and serve.

TULUMBA DESSERT
(SERVES 8)

INGREDIENTS

SYRUP:

3 cups confectioner's sugar
1.5 cups lemon juice
2.5 cups water

DOUGH:

1/2 cup butter
1 tbsp water
1.5 cups all-purpose flour
6 eggs
1 tsp salt
1 tsp of syrup
1.5 cups sunflower or corn oil for frying

PREPARATION:

First prepare the syrup. Place the sugar, lemon juice, and water in a large pan and heat, stirring continuously, until the sugar has completely dissolved. When the syrup is slightly tacky, remove from the heat and leave to cool.

While the syrup is cooling, melt the butter in a pan and heat until it sizzles. Add salt and water and bring back to the boil. Immediately pour in all of the flour and mix quickly into a dough. Reduce the heat, and beat the dough hard with a wooden spoon, turning it thoroughly. Remove from the heat and leave to cool.

When the dough is cool, work the eggs into the dough, one by one. Place the dough into a large icing bag with a wide, ridged nozzle (about 1 inch/2.5 cm).

Heat the sunflower or corn oil to a low to medium heat. From the icing bag, squeeze out 7–8 pieces of tulumba at a time into the warm sunflower oil. The pieces should be as thick as a finger and about 2 inches (4–5 cm) long. Once the tulumba begin to swell in the pan, increase the heat and cook them until light golden brown. Remove from the oil with a skimmer and drain of excess oils on kitchen paper. Place the cooked tulumba into the syrup.

When you have cooked all the tulumba and they have soaked up all the syrup, they are ready to serve.

Note: Before squeezing the dough out of the bag, make sure the oil is not too hot. If it is sizzling, you should let it cool down a little.

CHESTNUT DUMPLINGS
(SERVES 4 – 5)

INGREDIENTS

10 oz/250 g chestnut
1 cup confectioner's sugar
1 cup ground walnuts
1 cup raisins
10 vanilla wafers (or petites beurres), crushed
1 cup milk
1 tbsp crushed pistachios

CHOCOLATE SAUCE:

1 cup milk
1 cup water
1 tsp cornstarch
1 tsp all-purpose flour
1 tbsp cocoa
1 tbsp confectioner's sugar
1 egg yolk

PREPARATION:

Peel, boil and puree the chestnuts. Add the sugar, walnuts and raisins, cookies, and milk, then knead all together. Form the mixture into small balls, roll them in the crushed pistachios, and lay them out on a serving dish.

For the chocolate sauce, mix all the ingredients together in a mixing bowl or blender. Pour into a pan and cook over low heat, stirring constantly, until the mixture has thickened.

Pour over the dumplings and serve. Verser sur les boulettes et servir.

BAKED RICE PUDDING
(SERVES 6)

INGREDIENTS

1/2 cup pudding rice
2 pints/1 liter milk
1 cup confectioner's sugar
2 egg yolks
1.5 cups rice flour
1 tsp vanilla essence
salt

PREPARATION:

Cook the rice with 1.5 cups water and a pinch of salt. When the rice is tender, add the milk (reserving half a cup for later) and continue to simmer for 10 minutes. Add the sugar.

Blend the egg yolks, rice flour, and half a cup of milk together well. Take one ladle-full of the pudding that is simmering in the pan and blend with the egg and rice flour mix. Stir this mixture back into the pudding, blending well to avoid lumps. Stir in the vanilla essence.

Once the pudding has thickened, remove from the heat and place in an ovenproof glass dish. Stand this in a baking tray filled with water and bake until the top becomes golden brown.

Note: You may add a handful of seedless black raisins into the pudding before baking.

KUNAFA
(SERVES 4)

INGREDIENTS

8 oz/200 g kadayif
2 oz/50 g turkish "dil peyniri" or mozarella, thinly sliced
4 tbsp butter
14 oz /400 g sugar
2 cups water

PREPARATION:

Break the kadayif into short pieces and mix with 1.5 tablespoons of butter. Grease the base of a metal pie pan and spread with half of the kadayif and butter mix. Layer the sliced cheese on top. Make another layer with the rest of the kadayif.

Bake in a moderate oven (160 °C, 325 °F) until slightly golden. Remove the pie pan from the oven. With a spatula, flip the pastry over in the pan without breaking it, return it to the oven, and bake until the other side is golden too.

While the pastry is baking, make a thick, clear syrup by dissolving the sugar in water. Do not let the syrup caramelize. Leave to cool.

When the pastry is golden, remove it from the oven, and pour the cooled syrup over it. Serve in slices.

Note: Garnish with chopped nuts and serve with clotted cream.

MILKY PUMPKIN
(SERVES 6)

INGREDIENTS

3 lb/1.75 kg pumpkin
1 cup water
1 pint milk
2 cups sugar
2 tsps vanilla essence

GARNISH:

crushed hazelnuts, walnuts or coconut flakes
pomegranate seeds

PREPARATION:

Peel the pumpkin, remove the seeds, and slice. Wash with plenty of water and drain. Cook with a cup of water until it forms a puree.

Add the milk, sugar and vanilla essence and put through the blender. Next, return to the pan and cook on a low heat until it thickens and is quite stiff. Leave to cool and spoon into the serving dishes.

Sprinkle with nuts and pomegranate seeds before serving.

SERVER PASHA
(SERVES 6-8)

INGREDIENTS

8 oz/200 g french bread, crust removed
4 cups milk
3 eggs
1 tbsp confectioner's sugar
3 tbsp butter, melted

SYRUP:

1/4 cups confectioner's sugar
1 tsp lemon juice
1 cup water

PREPARATION:

Shred the French bread into bite-sized pieces, place in a large bowl, and pour the milk on top. Leave the bread to soak up the milk for about half an hour. Break the pieces up into even smaller bits. Add the eggs, confectioner's sugar and butter and knead for 5 minutes until the ingredients are blended well.

Spread this mixture on a greased baking tray, in a layer about one inch thick. Bake in a moderate oven (160 °C, 325 °F) heat for about an hour or until both the top and bottom of the mix has browned. If bubbles form during baking, pierce the bubble with a knife it.

Put the sugar, water and lemon juice in a pan. Cook over a low heat until the sugar dissolves, then bring to the boil and simmer for 15 more minutes until it thickens. (You should start to prepare the syrup about 20 minutes before removing the desert from the oven.)

After taking the desert out of the oven, pour the syrup over it. Once the dessert is completely cool, cut into small squares and serve.

SWEET DUMPLINGS (LOKMA)
(SERVES 6-8)

INGREDIENTS

2 cups all-purpose flour
1 cup of water in which garbanzo beans have been boiled
1 egg
1/3 cup milk
1 tsp powder yeast
1 tsp salt
1 tsp confectioner's sugar
2 pints/1 liter oil for frying

SYRUP:

3 cups confectioner's sugar
2 cups water
1 tsp lemon juice

PREPARATION:

First, make the syrup. Put the sugar and water into a pan and cook on a medium heat until the sugar dissolves. Simmer. When the syrup begins to thicken, add the lemon juice and bring to the boil again. Remove from the heat and leave to cool.

In a mixing bowl, put 1 and 1/3 cup flour. make a well in the centre. Into the well, pour an espresso cup of milk, 1 teaspoon of powder yeast, confectioner's sugar and salt. Knead the mixture well. Add the egg and knead some more. Then add the garbanzo bean water and knead again. Cover the dough and leave it to rise in a warm place.

Break the dough into small pieces using a lightly greased soup spoon and fry in hot oil. As the dumplings are cooked, remove from the oil and drain on kitchen paper.

Put the dumplings in the syrup. When they have soaked up the syrup, place on a serving dish and serve.

INDEX OF RECIPES